A CORNUCOPIA OF APHORISMS

Mahdy Y. Khaiyat

A CORNUCOPIA OF APHORISMS.

Copyright© 2012 by Mahdy Y. Khaiyat.

All rights reserved. No part of this book may be reproduced or transmitted in any form or by any means, electronic or mechanical without written permission from the publisher except in the case of brief quotations embodied in reviews and articles.

Published by M. K. Publishing.

P. O. Box 1265, Goleta, CA 93116 (805) 968-0040.
mahdy10@cox.net

Printed in the United States of America.

ISBN 978-0-9859188-0-4

FOREWORD

These aphorisms, whence they come, I do not know. They descend on me, like inspired angels, any time, any place I happen to be.

I hope you will be a beneficiary, too.

Aphorism: A short, pointed sentence containing some important truth or precept.

Webster's New Universal Dictionary of the English Language, Unabridged Edition, 1976.

Your birth is your path to extinction.

♦ ♦ ♦

For us humans, swallowing too many doses of reality is toxic; that is why we create endless holidays.

♦ ♦ ♦

The longer we cling to life, the better our chance to defeat death.

♦ ♦ ♦

Too much probing into reality causes us too much unhappiness.

♦ ♦ ♦

Let reality be undisturbed; now you may enjoy a fantasy of reality.

♦ ♦ ♦

Men love illusions; observe their reactions upon seeing a beautifully made-up woman.

♦ ♦ ♦

Keep a rosebud in your imagination; you will be surprised how fast it will grow and perfume your day and night.

♦ ♦ ♦

Virtue untamed is vice nourished.

♦ ♦ ♦

Familiarity bleeds creativity.

♦ ♦ ♦

Life is a fugitive enchantment.

♦ ♦ ♦

Beauty is a fleeting illusion.

♦ ♦ ♦

Poetry attempts to ferret out the mysterious in human behavior.

♦ ♦ ♦

Only a fool will believe that having more is having more security.

♦ ♦ ♦

If experience invalidates your thought, throw away any pretension of its usefulness.

♦ ♦ ♦

Adversities of living are many; experiences ought to condense them to a few.

♦ ♦ ♦

Imagination is the vinculum that ties knowledge and experience.

♦ ♦ ♦

Dark remains dark because one refuses to dilute it.

♦ ♦ ♦

Your soul may be your tormentor, but it is also your liberator.

♦ ♦ ♦

Swear allegiance to virtue even though vice may sometimes be imposed on you.

♦ ♦ ♦

Knowledge is a flower that flourishes— even in the dark!

♦ ♦ ♦

Knowledge begets knowledge.

♦ ♦ ♦

Power generates more power; unless moderated by morality, it will crush even the lowliest of its victims.

♦ ♦ ♦

Ignorance of the truth does not justify its violation.

♦ ♦ ♦

A belief nourished over time becomes a fact.

♦ ♦ ♦

In a sea of opulence, there is glaring indigence.

♦ ♦ ♦

When the mind is laden with such midden as
negative thoughts, it must be cleansed
with prayer or meditation.

♦ ♦ ♦

A rumor sustained over time becomes a fact.

♦ ♦ ♦

A failing man is no hypocrite when he advises
others not to fall into the same hole.

♦ ♦ ♦

A greedy person will always be greedy.

♦ ♦ ♦

Nothing is permanent but
the permanence of true love.

♦ ♦ ♦

Time may heal a youthful hurt, but for an older person there is no time.

♦ ♦ ♦

In solitude, the mind has plenitude to tell.

♦ ♦ ♦

Silence is a masterful language.

♦ ♦ ♦

You win an argument by showing, not telling.

♦ ♦ ♦

A reputation tarnished is a reputation lost.

♦ ♦ ♦

Society urges conformity; it is at its deadliest when it proclaims its love for you.

♦ ♦ ♦

The history of misery and the history of mirth suggest an internecine competition.

♦ ♦ ♦

If everyone born upholds the truth, life would be unbearably boring.

♦ ♦ ♦

For some of us, the path between ignoble and noble is long and arduous.

♦ ♦ ♦

Scoop what pleasures you can today, for tomorrow's offerings may be few and meager.

♦ ♦ ♦

Words that slip out of your lips cannot be recalled; and the consequences are incalculable.

♦ ♦ ♦

Genuine tears can move mountains.

♦ ♦ ♦

Writing poetry may be lonely, but it is lovely to discover pearls of wisdom while writing it.

♦ ♦ ♦

Time has soft touches, often with deadly effects.

♦ ♦ ♦

Hatred hurts and utter hatred hurts utterly.

♦ ♦ ♦

The quiet mind finds its way through
a maze of noise.

♦ ♦ ♦

The universe has not changed;
our perception of it has.

♦ ♦ ♦

Live and die by your own words.

♦ ♦ ♦

In the midst of this exquisite flower arrangement,
you are a thorn.

♦ ♦ ♦

Death is an indomitable equalizer.

♦ ♦ ♦

He who wishes to reach the highest glories must not fear heights.

♦ ♦ ♦

Insecurity engenders jealousy.

♦ ♦ ♦

Poets are forever grateful to Nature; she untiringly bestows her possessions upon them.

♦ ♦ ♦

A person who refuses to admit his mistakes is not ready to gain wisdom.

♦ ♦ ♦

Temperance develops through lengthy ruminations.

♦ ♦ ♦

In pride, we may hide our weaknesses.

♦ ♦ ♦

Undiscovered laws of nature may lie
just under your gaze.

♦ ♦ ♦

What a person lacks in resources,
he compensates with wits.

♦ ♦ ♦

When you are young, Time is an unending tunnel.

♦ ♦ ♦

Teach me a thing or two, and I am eternally
grateful to you.

♦ ♦ ♦

Be different, by design or by accident, and you are noticed.

♦ ♦ ♦

Pay no attention to details and you may be stranded in a vast ocean of trouble.

♦ ♦ ♦

Art is a distortion of reality, but it is a welcome distortion.

♦ ♦ ♦

In order for civilizations to flourish, they must stimulate intellectual activity.

♦ ♦ ♦

I feel, therefore I am human.

♦ ♦ ♦

As demonstrated by their behavior,
humans are both ugly and beautiful.

♦ ♦ ♦

A fanatic is one who insists that a rainbow has only
one color—his favorite one.

♦ ♦ ♦

Memory is a depository for safekeeping
the books of life.

♦ ♦ ♦

The ability to read is the ability to invent and
reinvent oneself—ad infinitum.

♦ ♦ ♦

Experience is what happens to you; wisdom is what
you do with the experience.

♦ ♦ ♦

Facts flash despite the intentional myopia.

♦ ♦ ♦

Too much passion degrades the mind.

♦ ♦ ♦

Poetry-writing is a process of self-recovery.

♦ ♦ ♦

Tyranny of traditions: Clenching onto traditions after it's proven they are detrimental to human dignity and progress.

♦ ♦ ♦

A giant of a man is one who can handle a major catastrophe as a tiny beast in the palm of his hand.

♦ ♦ ♦

Poetry is always looking for a suitable nest
to hatch its golden eggs.

♦ ♦ ♦

As currently practiced, free verse
is quintessentially formless.

♦ ♦ ♦

We try to define happiness and analyze it
intellectually, linguistically, and psychologically.
In the process, we feel unhappy, because we still
cannot find a satisfactory meaning of happiness. We
must abandon this effort since humans are able
to live without being happy.

♦ ♦ ♦

A poet lives in constant fear of a word or image
that refuses to land and take its appropriate place.

♦ ♦ ♦

I will do what I must; that is the supreme law
of survival.

♦ ♦ ♦

The soul's only worry is not to get caught
in a steely web of torment.

♦ ♦ ♦

Beauty is burdensome; the pressure to maintain it
despite the ravages of Time is unbearable.

♦ ♦ ♦

The womb of the universe keeps producing babies;
there is no sign that it will experience
a menopause any time soon.

♦ ♦ ♦

I fear a person with no moral principles; but I fear
more a person who has those principles
but keeps violating them.

♦ ♦ ♦

The proposition that man is a rational being is irrational; he is more emotional than rational; otherwise we would not be mired in such a mess.

♦ ♦ ♦

Sometimes when I see a beautiful woman walk down the street, I say to myself, "The Creator is emphatically more than perfect!"

♦ ♦ ♦

Old age: The human face is an archeological site.

♦ ♦ ♦

One's validity in life hinges on what one can offer.

♦ ♦ ♦

Those who wade only in life's shallows will never be able to swim in its depths.

◆ ◆ ◆

She is rich because she is loved; he is poor because he is not loved despite his riches.

◆ ◆ ◆

When I was younger I thought sex was the most important activity in my life; now that I am older, it is the most important thought in my life.

◆ ◆ ◆

Women love men because the former regard the latter as helpless children who want to be mothered whereas men love to take care of women. Period!

◆ ◆ ◆

He who has no enemies offers nothing of value.

♦ ♦ ♦

Men are often dragooned into marriage.

♦ ♦ ♦

We are often chained by our own acts.

♦ ♦ ♦

We are jettisoned onto this planet and there is no escape.

♦ ♦ ♦

I visited the future and I did not like what I saw; but I will pay a second visit.

♦ ♦ ♦

Power politics means showing the flag in your enemy's neighborhood—and getting away with it.

♦ ♦ ♦

Genuine patriotism is a noble feeling.

♦ ♦ ♦

He who invokes patriotism as a defense for his argument is on shaky ground.

♦ ♦ ♦

The most effective way to combat temptation is not to get exposed to it.

♦ ♦ ♦

Temptation may lead one to a ravine full of sewage.

♦ ♦ ♦

Romancing an unfeeling woman is like romancing a stone: Wasting time and energy hoping she will at least be considerate.

♦ ♦ ♦

Marriage: A treaty of appeasement

♦ ♦ ♦

History looks favorably on those
who favor it for guidance.

♦ ♦ ♦

Traveling in a straight line may lead you to your
intended destination, but deviating from
your planned route may unfold valuable
discoveries.

♦ ♦ ♦

Life may be suffocating; dreaming is like
opening windows to get fresh air.

♦ ♦ ♦

When a pit bull shows his teeth,
he is not smiling at you.

♦ ♦ ♦

Money is not the source of evil; it's you.

♦ ♦ ♦

Poetry is an inexhaustible source of spiritual wealth and beauty.

♦ ♦ ♦

There is no such thing as life without suffering, any more than a medicine without a side effect.

♦ ♦ ♦

A competent poet is one who borrows from another without being detected.

♦ ♦ ♦

A person who maintains silence may be gathering information—and scheming.

♦ ♦ ♦

Beware the ignorant ally.

♦ ♦ ♦

Maintain ambiguity; disclosure may precipitate your demise.

♦ ♦ ♦

If your enemy calls you names, do not retort by using the same, otherwise you stoop to his level.

♦ ♦ ♦

Trust those whom you can trust, but ask politely for verification.

♦ ♦ ♦

A good businessman always asks
for a signed contract.

♦ ♦ ♦

Education is subversion.

♦ ♦ ♦

Dreams review one's unfinished business.

♦ ♦ ♦

Skepticism is an integral part of the
search for knowledge.

♦ ♦ ♦

Lofty ambitions start with little dreams.

♦ ♦ ♦

He who claims to tell the truth all the time and under any circumstances without any reservation whatsoever, must have been born on an extinct planet or on one yet to be born.

♦ ♦ ♦

Freedom is not given; it is wrested from the jaws of oppressors.

♦ ♦ ♦

The destruction-construction nexus is as natural in human behavior as it is in nature.

♦ ♦ ♦

Nature's mammaries are indeed mammoth; they keep nourishing us as long as we reproduce.

♦ ♦ ♦

Admitting now one's limitations will save one considerable trouble later.

♦ ♦ ♦

Fastidious adherence to etiquette may be justifiable
when the appropriate occasions arise,
but adhering to it when unnecessary is enslaving.

♦ ♦ ♦

Do not envy someone who is above you in rank,
but sympathize with the one below yours.

♦ ♦ ♦

Flaunting your knowledge can create enemies as
well as admirers for you. The enemies are those
with weaker egos; the admirers are those anxious
to learn.

♦ ♦ ♦

If it is accepted that life is full of contradictions,
why do we continue to create more of them?

♦ ♦ ♦

If nothing else, suffering gives you a perspective
on how to deal more effectively
with your future experiences.

♦ ♦ ♦

Facts are not immutable.

♦ ♦ ♦

When you are elderly, you do not make hasty
judgments; consequences are always on your mind.

♦ ♦ ♦

Life's road hazards are many, but if you know your
path well, you do not need help
in reaching your destination.

♦ ♦ ♦

You are shaking my hand, but you remain distant.

♦ ♦ ♦

War: Humanity's perpetual scourge.

♦ ♦ ♦

Natural calamities are unnatural if we revere
Nature as a caring Mother.

♦ ♦ ♦

A person who has no system of beliefs
may not be able to sustain himself psychologically.

♦ ♦ ♦

An assault on character, based on truth or falsehood,
cannot be blunted or softened.

♦ ♦ ♦

Poetry is feeling wrapped in thought,
sung by songsters, memorized, and recited by
untold numbers.

♦ ♦ ♦

Entrenched in its habitat,
evil is difficult to ferret out.

♦ ♦ ♦

As long as you hold principles to be inviolable,
they will remain inviolable!

♦ ♦ ♦

Pleasing others requires self-denial.

♦ ♦ ♦

Boast not of your achievement;
if it is worth noticing, people will notice.

♦ ♦ ♦

You may be proud of your great deed, but others
may achieve even greater ones
which they consider only little deeds.

♦ ♦ ♦

A book is a powerful creature that
needs to be pampered and protected.

♦ ♦ ♦

Powerful words engender powerful reactions.

♦ ♦ ♦

He who keeps clutching his tribe is an infant
who refuses to be weaned.

♦ ♦ ♦

Opinions of others sediment in our subconscious;
they spring out later in life to assume our identity.

♦ ♦ ♦

Smile at those who tell you they are seeking their
paths; question those who claim
to have found theirs.

♦ ♦ ♦

Ponder the consequences before acting.

♦ ♦ ♦

Visit and revisit the past; you may be pleasantly
surprised by your new discoveries.

♦ ♦ ♦

In the midst of charting a strategy, it becomes clear
that there is no distinction between
offense and defense.

♦ ♦ ♦

Many wars are initiated by old politicians;
the young march to the drumbeats of patriotism.

♦ ♦ ♦

If truth and falsehood were assigned colors, the
former would choose white, the latter black.
White and black would merge to form the true color
of humanity.

♦ ♦ ♦

In its salacious form, sin is tempting and
scrumptious; some of us will be overwhelmed.

♦ ♦ ♦

When a poem is about to descend, I feverishly look
for all the appropriate words to their last syllables.

♦ ♦ ♦

Soul is illusive.

◆ ◆ ◆

Memory, memory,
spare me from any past disharmony.

◆ ◆ ◆

Don't despair! What is about to come may
be the best.

◆ ◆ ◆

If society is unfair to you, don't confront it head-on;
minimize its impact.

◆ ◆ ◆

I am wealthy because I don't have many things
that will make me poor one day.

◆ ◆ ◆

My health, my health, my health is my wealth—
and I am absolutely content.

♦ ♦ ♦

There is no known cure for entrenched pessimism.

♦ ♦ ♦

I wish I could go to a restaurant and order happiness; it must be a delicacy!

♦ ♦ ♦

My inalienable rights are also sacrosanct.

♦ ♦ ♦

Ignorance is pandemic, but curable.

♦ ♦ ♦

Sin is a departure from the straight line.

♦ ♦ ♦

Roses wilt sooner than mums—
a warning of the fragility of beauty.

♦ ♦ ♦

There is goodness in ugly things,
just as there is ugliness in good things.

♦ ♦ ♦

If the biblical system of justice such as a gouged
eye for a gouged eye is strictly applied now, pretty
soon we will have eyes piling up everywhere—
while eyeing us.

♦ ♦ ♦

Inebriated by ardent feelings of patriotism, we rush
to unnecessary wars; then we defend our behavior
using spurious reasoning.

♦ ♦ ♦

Coursing through history, it seems we are still sleep-walking our way to disaster after disaster.

♦ ♦ ♦

Human nature is immutable, claims to the contrary notwithstanding.

♦ ♦ ♦

Poetry writing: Fewer words, more meaning.

♦ ♦ ♦

By writing these thoughts, I do not aspire to be a prophet or a charlatan.

♦ ♦ ♦

What the future holds for you depends on what you have done today.

♦ ♦ ♦

Envy is a mental calamity.

♦ ♦ ♦

Hatred unchecked is hatred entrenched.

♦ ♦ ♦

What the ears hear may not coincide with what the eyes see.

♦ ♦ ♦

Our eyes meet; yours are brimming with our unsettled accounts.

♦ ♦ ♦

Life is a leaky boat; traveling in it is risky, but we keep traveling.

♦ ♦ ♦

Happiness is a state of mind and the mind states
what it wants, even at the cost of its happiness.

♦ ♦ ♦

Keep a turquoise rose in your fancy;
a beautiful woman may stop by and smile at you.

♦ ♦ ♦

Ignorance should not be deemed shameful;
no one knows everything.

♦ ♦ ♦

An unwanted change may turn out to be a blessing.

♦ ♦ ♦

Visit the past as often as you can;
more inspiration may be waiting for you.

♦ ♦ ♦

Keeping anger inside with no resolution
may create affliction.

♦ ♦ ♦

When you look at me the way you do,
a warm feeling waltzes through me.

♦ ♦ ♦

When you open a book you open possibilities
whose limits are set in the stratosphere and beyond.

♦ ♦ ♦

I am not sure if I can honestly recommend that you
adhere to your convictions regardless of the cost.
But if you do, you are a rare breed.

♦ ♦ ♦

Keep knocking on my door; if you are tired
of knocking, your visit is probably unnecessary.

♦ ♦ ♦

Slander: Poison gas against which there is no defense.

♦ ♦ ♦

Just as sea captains develop their reputations by weathering dangerous storms, political leaders develop theirs by surmounting political maelstroms.

♦ ♦ ♦

Be assertive in a crowd; assertiveness will yield incalculable benefits as you navigate life.

♦ ♦ ♦

It is a challenge to be frugal when you swim in a sea of plenty.

♦ ♦ ♦

Wisdom comes from questioning.

♦ ♦ ♦

The central tenet of nationalism: The defense of one's country and its ideals overrides all other considerations.

♦ ♦ ♦

Sometimes we travel long distances to find the truth, but in all likelihood it stands before our eyes.

♦ ♦ ♦

Death dares not come near you—until it's time.

♦ ♦ ♦

When we leave this earth, we sadly leave behind things we do not wish to.

♦ ♦ ♦

Invisible wounds can be more hurtful
than visible ones.

♦ ♦ ♦

A vast ocean is like a vast desert:
Each offers opportunities as well as problems.

♦ ♦ ♦

Partial answers keep you wondering—
and wandering and wandering.

♦ ♦ ♦

Show your humility whenever you can,
for in humility there is inner peace.

♦ ♦ ♦

An unrestrained ambition is a catastrophe
waiting to happen.

♦ ♦ ♦

Weakness invites more weakness.

♦ ♦ ♦

On balance, it is better to be thoughtful than thoughtless.

♦ ♦ ♦

War of attrition: Another phrase for a test of wills.

♦ ♦ ♦

Abuses committed in the name of religion abuse that religion.

♦ ♦ ♦

As mankind thrives, so do wars.

♦ ♦ ♦

Dreams are antidotes to loneliness.

♦ ♦ ♦

Atheism: Belief in disbelief.

♦ ♦ ♦

Women are not inferior; look how low men sink to win them!

♦ ♦ ♦

The thorns on the stem of the rose warn of the cost of desiring beauty.

♦ ♦ ♦

The greatest danger in being in love is to continue paying tribute to its remains.

♦   ♦   ♦

In wars, the dead are the luckiest!

♦   ♦   ♦

Wisdom comes from questioning.

♦   ♦   ♦

Humanity asserts: I feel before I think.

♦   ♦   ♦

As soon as you hit the ground, stay there awhile; you will see the world in a different perspective.

♦   ♦   ♦

At first blush, zigzagging and meandering may be taken as erratic behavior. In fact, it may be a method of exploration and discovery.
Traveling in a straight line is predictable.

♦ ♦ ♦

Art never accepts stability; it is a revolutionary process that seeks to undermine what is acceptable.

♦ ♦ ♦

Paleontology: Nature's Lost and Found Department where heirlooms can be examined and claimed without probate.

♦ ♦ ♦

Altruism is an extension of egoism.

♦ ♦ ♦

Wealth is a nest of snake eggs.
Watch out when they hatch!

♦ ♦ ♦

There is nothing more stirring than the image of
a kitten sitting in your palm while
her wide-open eyes are staring at you.

♦ ♦ ♦

I have discovered that life offers both love and
hatred; it is your choice.

♦ ♦ ♦

Expect nothing from the world and
you will live as happily as you expect.

♦ ♦ ♦

Expect the unexpected
and you will live anxiety-free.

♦ ♦ ♦

Poetry that elicits different interpretations
is great poetry.

♦ ♦ ♦

It is better to have little and enjoy it than have much and not enjoy it.

♦ ♦ ♦

Let there be justice, let there be light.

♦ ♦ ♦

Justice denied, justice decried.

♦ ♦ ♦

Death is not your garden-variety military dictator; he is an unrepentant field marshal of blood and gore.

♦ ♦ ♦

Death recognizes no boundaries; it does not even carry a travel document.

♦ ♦ ♦

Heavily made-up, she says, "It's natural to be unnatural when you reach a certain age."

♦ ♦ ♦

We are afraid of the dark because of what it represents.

♦ ♦ ♦

Death does not offer a smile, only a bludgeon.

♦ ♦ ♦

Imitating a writer you admire may suppress your unique individuality.

♦ ♦ ♦

If you interpret my tolerance as weakness, you are in for a big surprise.

♦ ♦ ♦

History offers both support and criticism.

♦ ♦ ♦

I find truth in beauty, and beauty in truth.

♦ ♦ ♦

Exercising power over another, under dubious pretexts, is morally reprehensible.

♦ ♦ ♦

A winner is one who does not complain when severely tested.

♦ ♦ ♦

Poetry will never be irrelevant—
unless humans become irrelevant.

♦ ♦ ♦

Every culture has its heroes, but one culture's hero may be another culture's villain.

♦ ♦ ♦

You may think your opinions are superior to your supervisor's, but your supervisor can convert his into policies.

♦ ♦ ♦

Enjoying liberty without the commitment to defend it is cowardice of the first order.

♦ ♦ ♦

Your heart is made of asphalt; let me help you repair some of your potholes.

♦ ♦ ♦

It is not shameful to possess platinum and diamonds; what is shameful is to squirrel them away while the needy die of hunger.

♦ ♦ ♦

We are immortalized by what we leave behind.

♦ ♦ ♦

If all our wishes were fulfilled, we would have nothing to complain about and nothing to hope for.

♦ ♦ ♦

Beware of throwing criticisms around; they may boomerang on you.

♦ ♦ ♦

You cannot impose wisdom on people; they have to seek it.

♦ ♦ ♦

While making your journey, your path may be strewn with broken emotions; carry on even though you have to limp.

♦ ♦ ♦

What separates men from other men is the degree of commitment to good moral principles.

♦ ♦ ♦

Whether you admit it or not, sometimes you are as ignorant as I am.

♦ ♦ ♦

Believe and let believe—and disbelieve.

♦ ♦ ♦

Religion should welcome and guide, not reject and misguide.

♦ ♦ ♦

My mind is my temple; you may tap on the door if
you wish entry, otherwise, continue
your journey unescorted.

♦ ♦ ♦

Self-control, like patience, has limits.

♦ ♦ ♦

To err is an absolute right;
to repeatedly err is an absolute incompetence.

♦ ♦ ♦

Behind every successful comedian is a tragedy.

♦ ♦ ♦

Tears tear through me when I write a tearfully terrifying poem.

♦ ♦ ♦

How to subdue a cantankerous poem: Just love her, simply love her.

♦ ♦ ♦

I crossed the bridge less crossed and I ended up in a ravine.

♦ ♦ ♦

On the tombstone: Here lies an unfinished aphorism.

♦ ♦ ♦

Mankind: Work in progress.

♦ ♦ ♦

Lamppost: A monument that enlightens a dark world.

♦ ♦ ♦

Abraham Lincoln was murdered in cold blood, but his hot blood still flows in our veins.

♦ ♦ ♦

True love lives truthfully; untrue love untruthfully.

♦ ♦ ♦

To behave young when old will help you slow your movement to the precipice.

♦ ♦ ♦

New ideas are always opposed because they violate the sanctity of the old.

♦ ♦ ♦

An aphorist comes up with a thought,
the reader with an interpretation.

♦   ♦   ♦

Like a florist, an aphorist arranges his words
and meanings in an exquisite bouquet.

♦   ♦   ♦

Where do verses and ideas come from?
Mostly from the subconscious mind.

♦   ♦   ♦

Time is corrosive; that is why we need
a blacksmith!

♦   ♦   ♦

With the help of his demolition crew,
Time deconstructs what nature constructs.

♦ ♦ ♦

Individually we are nothing;
collectively everything.

♦ ♦ ♦

A friend tells me these thoughts are not mine;
I am only the medium.

♦ ♦ ♦

Oh, the price humanity pays for liberty.

♦ ♦ ♦

Liberty lost is life lost.

♦ ♦ ♦

If you think you're not a great poet, you probably
are not.

♦ ♦ ♦

What is great poetry? Reading it creates immediate emotional and intellectual agitation.

♦ ♦ ♦

Power intoxicates even a teetotaler!

♦ ♦ ♦

Laws devoid of morality cannot last.

♦ ♦ ♦

Wealth provides comfort and convenience, seldom tranquility and happiness.

♦ ♦ ♦

Given the existence of unlimited destructive weapons and given the fragility and insanity of humanity, the coming world war would mutate us into extinction.

♦ ♦ ♦

Life is a splendid melancholy.

♦ ♦ ♦

It is always desirable to look at the peak of the mountain, even if you are unable to reach it.

♦ ♦ ♦

Behind a successful action
there is a successful thought.

♦ ♦ ♦

What is mesmerizing about life is that it represents itself as such.

♦ ♦ ♦

I belong to all and all belongs to me.

♦ ♦ ♦

A rose secures her future by what she offers today:
Memories of those who cosset her.

♦ ♦ ♦

The challenge is to recognize beauty
without seeing it.

♦ ♦ ♦

Democracy: Its defenders trumpet that it is
a peaceful system which goes to extremes only
when it's threatened.

♦ ♦ ♦

Be outgoing, but keep a little corner
for introspection.

♦ ♦ ♦

One writes poetry because one is tired of writing straightforwardly and unambiguously as in prose.

♦ ♦ ♦

I do not keep a library; I tap on the door of my imagination and a cornucopia of ideas, images, and words spill out.

♦ ♦ ♦

Silence is provocative.

♦ ♦ ♦

We fear what we do not know and know our fear is irrational or even pathological.

♦ ♦ ♦

Thoughtfulness is a human trait, but excessive
thoughtfulness can be dangerous because
it can be misinterpreted.

◆ ◆ ◆

When a dictator hears a chant of support for him,
he hears an approaching danger; he knows
that chant is not spontaneous.

◆ ◆ ◆

Life is a struggle without end—
interspersed with a lace of sweetness.

◆ ◆ ◆

Beware! A thorough self-analysis may lead
to self-immolation.

◆ ◆ ◆

Sooner or later, the cloud of death will hover
on your sunset.

♦ ♦ ♦

A man and a woman can form a close non-sexual relationship—provided they are both unambiguously and unacceptably unattractive.

♦ ♦ ♦

In order to win, you must be proactively engaged.

♦ ♦ ♦

Soliloquy: A manner of speaking.

♦ ♦ ♦

Education can be used for good or evil.

♦ ♦ ♦

Only the purpose-driven life is worth living.

♦ ♦ ♦

The audacity of change: Shake off the yoke of decaying conventions and start celebrating your rebirth.

♦ ♦ ♦

World government will never be accepted because of the loss of national sovereignties.

♦ ♦ ♦

Demand excellence in everything you do; mediocrity is poverty.

♦ ♦ ♦

Moderation in thought must be matched by moderation in behavior.

♦ ♦ ♦

Cliché is the antithesis of creativity.

♦ ♦ ♦

You gain experience and knowledge
even though you are bed-ridden.

♦ ♦ ♦

True knowledge can only come through experience.

♦ ♦ ♦

Beauty is mortal, but its impact is immortal.

♦ ♦ ♦

One may be denied access to knowledge,
but not to imagination.

♦ ♦ ♦

A one-sided civility cannot last long.

♦ ♦ ♦

I may not succeed in writing these sentences aphoristically, but if you understand them, my job is done.

♦ ♦ ♦

Middle age crisis is like stopping your voyage midstream and feeling lost.

♦ ♦ ♦

Eat, sleep, and be merry as long as you use your brains.

♦ ♦ ♦

Our feelings originate in our brains, not our hearts.

♦ ♦ ♦

Let the unspoken idea stay in your depths and ferment. When it's ready, let it bubble to the surface like fine wine.

♦ ♦ ♦

Work of art: I discover something new every time I look at it.

♦ ♦ ♦

A fire hydrant is a dog's best friend.

♦ ♦ ♦

A good diplomat never comments on anything directly.

♦ ♦ ♦

A bank is a sanctuary for your fleeing dollars.

♦ ♦ ♦

A bank remains your friend as long as your deposits keep coming in.

♦ ♦ ♦

Money is an instrument of production.

♦ ♦ ♦

You can dissolve my body, but you cannot dissolve my thoughts and principles.

♦ ♦ ♦

My suffering will haunt you long after I am gone—assuming you have some humanity left.

♦ ♦ ♦

Communication is power.

♦ ♦ ♦

In the beginning there was nothing; in the end there will be nothing.

♦ ♦ ♦

You may say your feelings reside in your heart as long as you concede that your heart resides in your cranium.

♦ ♦ ♦

There is the grandeur of the sea and there is the majesty of the sky; nothing else comes close.

♦ ♦ ♦

One must respect the lowliest among us; they have their own stories to tell, too.

♦ ♦ ♦

When wealth alone sustains your self-respect, its loss can be fatal.

♦ ♦ ♦

Discipline! Discipline! Everything else will fall in place.

♦ ♦ ♦

Your positive attitude helps dissolve this pitch dark night.

♦ ♦ ♦

A positive attitude saves the day.

♦ ♦ ♦

What is beauty but the flowering of the self.

♦ ♦ ♦

Truth is more beautiful than fiction.

♦ ♦ ♦

Receiving respect from others requires giving them the same.

♦ ♦ ♦

Showing your own self-respect induces others to give you theirs.

♦ ♦ ♦

Where logic fails to take its place, sentimentalism flourishes.

♦ ♦ ♦

What makes man human is his capacity to create and endure tragedies.

♦ ♦ ♦

Man's capacity to commit evil can only be surpassed by his propensity to do good.

♦ ♦ ♦

I hope, therefore I exist.

♦ ♦ ♦

Self-knowledge is a life-long process.

♦ ♦ ♦

The best leader is one who leads least.

♦ ♦ ♦

Maintaining your composure while under attack defines your character.

♦ ♦ ♦

Age is a testament to life-long accomplishments.

♦ ♦ ♦

Man is the only animal who makes
and breaks promises.

♦ ♦ ♦

Tact is the ability to weasel out of
a difficult situation without being noticed.

♦ ♦ ♦

Cynics know how to spoil your day: They accuse
you of being too optimistic.

♦ ♦ ♦

Be a humanitarian just for one day and
the world will be saved!

♦ ♦ ♦

The human race will probably be extinct;
we just don't know when.

♦ ♦ ♦

Nothing tempts like temptation.

♦ ♦ ♦

There are many social ills but few social skills
to deal with them.

♦ ♦ ♦

When you say that a person has no morals, you
actually intend to say his morals
are incompatible with yours.

♦ ♦ ♦

Adults and children enjoyed flying kites,
but only Franklin saw the light.

♦ ♦ ♦

Old age has a way with tactics: It creeps up on you
when you are oblivious of his whereabouts.

♦ ♦ ♦

Lovers' moment: When words cease to exist.

♦ ♦ ♦

In the steely grip of death, you are no longer able to sip your favorite cup of optimism.

♦ ♦ ♦

The use of imprecise words and meanings often leads to imprecise thoughts and confusion.

♦ ♦ ♦

The rewards of good education cannot be overestimated.

♦ ♦ ♦

Your work is your organizer; you always go back to it whenever you feel lost.

♦ ♦ ♦

Emotions unfettered are catastrophes galloping to the abyss.

♦ ♦ ♦

The authenticity of true love can only be ascertained over time.

♦ ♦ ♦

Life is a perennial laboratory.

♦ ♦ ♦

What is love but a path of wounds trodden by the hapless?

♦ ♦ ♦

Such love is found in the fiery fulfillment
of the moment.

♦ ♦ ♦

Feminine intuition discerns what cannot be
discerned by ordinary means.

♦ ♦ ♦

Distaff: The eccentricities of femaleness.

♦ ♦ ♦

If you cannot swim, you cannot jump into the
deep ocean for a second time.

♦ ♦ ♦

East and West: An artificial division—they come
from the same womb and they will return
to the same womb.

♦ ♦ ♦

When science and spiritual depth travel together, the distance to the destination is shortened.

♦ ♦ ♦

When conscience is stifled, civilization hemorrhages.

♦ ♦ ♦

Conscience: A warning mechanism of an imminent embarrassing discovery.

♦ ♦ ♦

Conscience: A whining watch dog.

♦ ♦ ♦

Reality! Reality! The irrepressible Monster!

♦ ♦ ♦

Fame can drag you to places you do not want to be.

♦ ♦ ♦

I do not wish to be in the limelight;
I only wish my aphorisms were.

♦ ♦ ♦

To surrender to temptation is foolish because
you do not know what it harbors.

♦ ♦ ♦

I wish I could attend a reunion of all the inner
characters who took the liberty of representing me
over the years.

♦ ♦ ♦

The difference between science and religion:
Science is constantly developing;
religion, constantly sleeping.

♦ ♦ ♦

Once in a while, let your mind be disengaged
from the world—allow it to recuperate.

♦ ♦ ♦

Your thoughts, inimical or friendly, come through
by the words you use.

♦ ♦ ♦

Telling the truth or untruth entails consequences.

♦ ♦ ♦

Expect nothing from the world, and you will live
with great tranquility.

♦ ♦ ♦

Beauty is cleavage-deep.

♦ ♦ ♦

Standing beside successful men
are supportive women.

♦ ♦ ♦

Fear not of the unknown; it may be carrying
a basket of gold nuggets.

♦ ♦ ♦

Instead of telling the world you're carrying carrots
and a big stick, show them you're carrying plenty
of carrots and flowers; the reaction will amaze you.

♦ ♦ ♦

By stirring up the dust of curiosity, you may be
stirring up the cloud of anxiety.

♦ ♦ ♦

Nothing is certain but uncertainty.

♦ ♦ ♦

Look into the eye of the disaster and gouge it before it can reach you.

♦ ♦ ♦

The mind is a wondrous instrument.

♦ ♦ ♦

The sound of silence is deafening.

♦ ♦ ♦

The march and sound of positive thinking: Yes, we can! Yes, we can! Yes, we can!— ad infinitum.

♦ ♦ ♦

We are on Earth to fulfill a supreme purpose;
it is up to us to keep it supreme.

♦ ♦ ♦

Death: The cessation of involuntary activity on Earth and the start of another in St. Nowhere.

♦ ♦ ♦

The weak cry injustice; the powerful continue the injustice.

♦ ♦ ♦

Placebo: The triumph of deception.

♦ ♦ ♦

Invisible wounds tend to resist healing.

♦ ♦ ♦

Groupthink: Choosing collective security over independent thinking and responsibility.

♦ ♦ ♦

The birth of humanity was the birth of tragedy, or comedy clothed in tragedy.

♦ ♦ ♦

It is better to be in doubt than be surprised by certainty.

♦ ♦ ♦

Home is a sacrosanct sanctuary.

♦ ♦ ♦

It is permissible to allow oneself to be a fool once in a while, just to experience what fools go through every day.

♦ ♦ ♦

I am an incurable idealist, but succumb to realism when the odds against me are overwhelming.

♦ ♦ ♦

Water: Calm beauty, life saver, life terminator.

♦ ♦ ♦

When we seek friends, we really seek approval. This is perilous, since friendships can dissolve.

♦ ♦ ♦

A human being is rational and emotional; he is happiest when he is able to maintain this balance.

♦ ♦ ♦

Poise: Public speaking absent butterflies.

♦ ♦ ♦

Give a gun its rightful place; dump it.

♦ ♦ ♦

In one way or another, literary works are autobiographical.

♦ ♦ ♦

On acquiring knowledge: There is a parrot in all of us.

♦ ♦ ♦

The philosopher's advice: Know thyself. Absolutely not—self-knowledge is one of the scariest of experiences!

♦ ♦ ♦

If you are newly in love, you are on shaky ground.

♦ ♦ ♦

The raging fire of love cannot be extinguished with vague promises of fulfillment.

♦ ♦ ♦

Should I fear more someone with a brutal calculation of ambition or an unpredictable dishonest friend?

♦ ♦ ♦

A flower may wilt physically, but its spiritual essence will survive, even thrive.

♦ ♦ ♦

To ascertain the truth, one writes fiction.

♦ ♦ ♦

Everyone appreciated exotic animals and plants, but only Darwin knew their origins.

♦ ♦ ♦

Radical cases require radical measures.

♦ ♦ ♦

Be patient and the world will be patient with you; be impatient and the world will be impatient with you.

♦ ♦ ♦

Intimacy is the cornerstone of a durable relationship.

♦ ♦ ♦

Don't be ashamed of your mistakes; be ashamed
if you fail to correct them.

♦ ♦ ♦

Sudden fame can spoil your day

♦ ♦ ♦

Sudden riches can spoil your tranquility.

♦ ♦ ♦

He who is able to imagine has an unlimited future;
he who learns only what he is told, is content
with his future.

♦ ♦ ♦

UFO: Celestial visitors probing
for tellurian possibilities.

♦ ♦ ♦

Consuming too much protein may lead
to intellectual constipation.

♦ ♦ ♦

Consuming a balanced diet may lead
to erudition and enlightenment.

♦ ♦ ♦

Meanings of words are descriptions
of prior experiences.

♦ ♦ ♦

Beware of honey-coated words; they can be lethal.

♦ ♦ ♦

The aim of education is to reaffirm what is true
and to root out what is untrue.

♦ ♦ ♦

The proverbial battle of the sexes is actually a loud amorous argumentation between lovers on how best to achieve a satisfactory climax.

♦ ♦ ♦

Your work is your path to salvation.

♦ ♦ ♦

You are worth what you think you are worth.

♦ ♦ ♦

Podiatrist: A specialist who tries to persuade his patients to be footloose.

♦ ♦ ♦

With my parents deceased, I am a living repository of their histories.

♦ ♦ ♦

Brutal events in my life left their brutal marks on me with brutal efficiency.

♦ ♦ ♦

Since we are all going to die, why should we make the effort to keep ourselves alive?

♦ ♦ ♦

Ultimately, the universe is beyond our comprehension.

♦ ♦ ♦

Justice is what the conqueror says it is.

♦ ♦ ♦

Since time is inextricably linked to one's life, enjoy the remaining moments with decadent abandon.

♦ ♦ ♦

The birth of these heifers assures the continuation of human species.

♦ ♦ ♦

In order to write well, a writer must be an avid reader.

♦ ♦ ♦

Books are vehicles in perpetual motion carrying the products of our notions and imaginations.

♦ ♦ ♦

Subtle beauty is initially hard to discern, but when it becomes discernible, it will take you to a realm known only to a few.

♦ ♦ ♦

If life were fair, man should be allowed to choose
to live forever!

♦ ♦ ♦

Memory is unfillable storage.

♦ ♦ ♦

To the acutely curious mind, the ordinarily
indecipherable becomes the ordinarily decipherable.

♦ ♦ ♦

One goes to the theater to see a staged tragedy and
soon discovers that one's personal tragedy
is a lot more bearable.

♦ ♦ ♦

Strive to be good all the time; this is the least
that you can do as an individual.

♦ ♦ ♦

It is dangerous to be perceived as weak.

♦ ♦ ♦

Nationalism: When the flag is hoisted, insanity replaces sanity.

♦ ♦ ♦

Monarchy: An anachronistic system which aspires to achieve the status of divinity.

♦ ♦ ♦

Democracy: Where the majority votes and the minority rules.

♦ ♦ ♦

Socialism: You deserve what you strive for.

♦ ♦ ♦

Words are crutches that help you negotiate
life's mazes.

♦ ♦ ♦

If you really want to know someone,
do not listen to him; watch his behavior.

♦ ♦ ♦

When you run out of money, it is a practical
problem. When you run out of friends,
you have no one to help you nurse your wounds.

♦ ♦ ♦

A good poem awakens what is dormant in you.

♦ ♦ ♦

He who has few possessions will not lose sleep
over their loss.

♦ ♦ ♦

The crab's meanderings are instinctual
as a cock's crows.

♦ ♦ ♦

There is an affinity between a drunk and a crab:
They both cannot walk on a straight line.

♦ ♦ ♦

In the midst of suffering: The world of nonchalance
is thriving.

♦ ♦ ♦

Humanity's scourge: The bombs and the rockets
release their deadly contents on the innocents.

♦ ♦ ♦

Some of these aphorisms contradict each other.
Select one that is most appropriate at the time.

♦ ♦ ♦

Not a dozen or a hundred or even a thousand men
can stop an ignited passion from
pursuing its course.

♦ ♦ ♦

In our desperation to keep alive, we often accept a
medicine that is more dangerous than the disease.

♦ ♦ ♦

Your obnoxious behavior may be forgiven;
you are senile.

♦ ♦ ♦

Sometimes what you see does not wish to be seen.

♦ ♦ ♦

All this kerfuffle about nothing!

♦ ♦ ♦

The fish and the hook: It opens its mouth—
an open invitation to death.

♦ ♦ ♦

He who stands on the ground cannot voluntarily
fall onto the ground.

♦ ♦ ♦

Yes, I may be wise, but I lead a dull life.

♦ ♦ ♦

We create rules which sustain us;
then they rule and oppress us.

♦ ♦ ♦

Genuine repentance is commendable;
sham repentance regrettable

♦ ♦ ♦

It's up to you to defy the world, but you risk
being ostracized.

♦ ♦ ♦

Lack of self-esteem is the root of all violence.

♦ ♦ ♦

Self-love precedes love for others.

♦ ♦ ♦

If love is to survive, one must work
to keep it alive and vibrant.

♦ ♦ ♦

Hazards of living cannot be overstated.

♦ ♦ ♦

Education is not stuffing your mind with facts and statistics; rather it is learning to analyze concepts critically and synthesize them
into meaningful wholes.

♦ ♦ ♦

What separates atheism from theism is the letter A. It is thisclose physically, but their meanings constitute such an immeasurable gulf.

♦ ♦ ♦

A word of wisdom can be countered by another word of wisdom.

♦ ♦ ♦

Often, big words deliver small punches;
small words, potent blows.

♦ ♦ ♦

The root cause of all grief in stock investing
is greed.

♦ ♦ ♦

I don't have children; is this a blessing in disguise
or a disguise for something else?

♦ ♦ ♦

We are on this planet to help with its upkeep,
not its destruction.

♦ ♦ ♦

I stood on solid ground until temptation loosened
the soil beneath.

♦ ♦ ♦

The predictable thing about mankind
is its unpredictability.

♦ ♦ ♦

What does a stupid, self-admiring person see when
he looks into the mirror?
A stupid, self-admiring person, of course.

♦ ♦ ♦

Every human being is a book; it's up to you how to
read its words, interpret its sentences,
appreciate its messages, and adopt its wisdom.

♦ ♦ ♦

Tragedy is not knowing you're stupid.

♦ ♦ ♦

Seize the truth here and now; don't let loose.

♦ ♦ ♦

If you have no ambition to travel above your level,
no amount of encouragement can change that.

♦ ♦ ♦

Truth, like fact, stands opposed to its manipulations
and distortions.

♦ ♦ ♦

Memory is a dog that never tires of barking.

♦ ♦ ♦

Time: You can spend it, but you cannot hoard it.

♦ ♦ ♦

Free expression of thought is as natural
as having functioning vocal cords.

♦ ♦ ♦

Hope is the most effective weapon
of the downtrodden.

♦ ♦ ♦

Give and you will get—eventually.

♦ ♦ ♦

Tell the truth, the unadulterated truth, the total truth;
otherwise, you're suspected
of withholding fragments thereof.

♦ ♦ ♦

The distance between life and death is not vast, but
the distance between death and the thereafter
remains unknown.

♦ ♦ ♦

Letting anger fester is like clutching a flaming knife and stabbing your brain with it over and over again.

♦ ♦ ♦

The art of lying and the science of mnemonics must be studied together.

♦ ♦ ♦

Beauty–inner and external–attracts beauty.

♦ ♦ ♦

Traditional marriage: Serial monogamy.

♦ ♦ ♦

Beware a person who habitually agrees with you.

♦ ♦ ♦

When traumatized, write a poem;
its emollient effects will amaze you.

♦ ♦ ♦

Victory and defeat both offer their own challenges.

♦ ♦ ♦

Deprive someone of hope and you will kill
a worthy talent.

♦ ♦ ♦

I defend your liberty if you defend mine; if this
solemn agreement holds, our world will
forever be free.

♦ ♦ ♦

Ego and truth do not get along.

♦ ♦ ♦

Your opponents are eagerly
waiting for your mistakes.

♦ ♦ ♦

Wisdom eventually becomes a cliché.

♦ ♦ ♦

What we receive without effort,
we want to continue.

♦ ♦ ♦

As soon as you accept the idea that you're
exceptionalist, your existential burdens multiply.

♦ ♦ ♦

What happens behind closed doors is nobody's
concern; what happens outside,
becomes everyone else's agony or pleasure.

♦ ♦ ♦

Not everyone wants to confront the truth head-on.

♦ ♦ ♦

Humor is the oil that helps the cogs of life
turn more smoothly.

♦ ♦ ♦

Stupidity is a self-inflicted wound.

♦ ♦ ♦

The rumor that I have been elevated to the throne of
high poetry is prematurely conceived—
and incalculably painful.

♦ ♦ ♦

Beware! History is as watchful as ever.

♦ ♦ ♦

Life is illogic: To logicize it is to deny its essence.

♦ ♦ ♦

The diamond rule: Enjoy this life's enchanting lure before it dims in your twilight.

♦ ♦ ♦

Poet of Peace: When he emerges from the shadows, the world will be illumined.

♦ ♦ ♦

Verbal calisthenics will strengthen your language skills.

♦ ♦ ♦

What I am about, you're not about to know.

♦ ♦ ♦

Feelings and thoughts are two pillars
of the same edifice.

♦ ♦ ♦

The eye is a surveillance tool.

♦ ♦ ♦

Evil people remain evil because their styles obscure
their true selves.

♦ ♦ ♦

Leadership is the ability to induce others to do
things they would not otherwise do,
and do them every time.

♦ ♦ ♦

Self-acceptance is a prelude to acceptance of you
by others.

♦ ♦ ♦

Truth gets lost in the shuffle.

♦ ♦ ♦

Freedom of expression cannot be suspended just because our enemies take advantage of it.

♦ ♦ ♦

Survival of the best and the worst; together they form the just society.

♦ ♦ ♦

Fairness: Identical treatment for identical cases.

♦ ♦ ♦

Indecision is a form of decision.

♦ ♦ ♦

Gossiping may enhance camaraderie, but it can also spread falsehoods and injure reputations.

♦ ♦ ♦

Any limitation imposed on creativity is unforgivable cruelty.

♦ ♦ ♦

For a civilization to continue flourishing, it must view change as an integral part of its existence.

♦ ♦ ♦

A good book of life and a good book of death to read—the twain can never be separated.

♦ ♦ ♦

If we had the likes of Mother Theresa everywhere, we would no longer need philosophers and opinion manipulators.

♦ ♦ ♦

Without vice, there is no virtue and vice versa.

♦ ♦ ♦

Power and humility are as miscible as water and electricity.

♦ ♦ ♦

Conflict resolution: You gain enormously by using calming words rather than words that flatten a muscular giant.

♦ ♦ ♦

The existence of evil is a necessary evil; otherwise we won't strive for moral perfection.

♦ ♦ ♦

You fall prey to the fangs of death only once.

♦ ♦ ♦

The paradox of knowledge: In the illimitable space
of knowledge, the more one learns,
the less one knows.

♦ ♦ ♦

Marriage is a state of mind.

♦ ♦ ♦

Emotionally-charged words are more fearsome
than rockets and bombs.

♦ ♦ ♦

Trust in humanity, but keep watch over
your possessions.

♦ ♦ ♦

We are more entranced by physical than spiritual
beauty because we are influenced
by the immediate evidence.

♦ ♦ ♦

Success is the ability to adapt to
changing circumstances.

♦ ♦ ♦

The mammoth bridges we are building seem
insufficient to narrow the widening gap
in humanity.

♦ ♦ ♦

You can create your own inner paradise even
though you are in the midst of misery.

♦ ♦ ♦

We have no control over the whims of winds.
Be patient, even winds get tired at some point.

♦ ♦ ♦

The cloud may obscure the Sun, but we create our
own sun by penetrating the cloud of doubt.

♦ ♦ ♦

There is no such thing as art for art's sake;
there must be motivation of some kind.

♦ ♦ ♦

We all breathe the same air, but not all of us
appreciate its role in our lives.

♦ ♦ ♦

Say a giant "NO" to bigotry;
sing a mammoth "YES" to tolerance.

♦ ♦ ♦

Occasional suffering reminds us
of our vulnerability.

♦ ♦ ♦

There is no avoiding being hopeful;
otherwise you're not breathing.

♦ ♦ ♦

What is impossible may turn out to be possible,
allowing a journey of possibilities to continue.

♦ ♦ ♦

In order for seduction to succeed, the participants
must pay equal attention to each other's moves.

♦ ♦ ♦

We talk about happiness so much
as if nothing else matters.

♦ ♦ ♦

Once they are out, words cannot be recalled.

♦ ♦ ♦

Committing to a simple lifestyle is more satisfactory than a life full of material riches—and agonies

♦ ♦ ♦

Violence breeds violence breeds nonchalance toward life.

♦ ♦ ♦

Keep me in this earthly bliss; send me not to the fabled paradise.

♦ ♦ ♦

Shooting wars start with verbal battles.

♦ ♦ ♦

It is a mite hubristic to assert that human life
is more than a passing cloud.

♦ ♦ ♦

When the machine fails, science may be to blame;
when science is found sound, humans are to blame

♦ ♦ ♦

You are sandwiched between Heaven and Hades.
It's up to you to extricate yourself
from this predicament.

♦ ♦ ♦

Possessiveness is a calamity.

♦ ♦ ♦

More laws mean more chances to violate them.

♦ ♦ ♦

He who wishes to ruminate must first regurgitate what he swallows.

♦ ♦ ♦

Self-discovery is what you now know about yourself that everyone else has known for a long time.

♦ ♦ ♦

Biology is agony.

♦ ♦ ♦

History is judgmental, and he is not shy about it.

♦ ♦ ♦

There is nothing more important than the
importance you attach to your dignity
and self-esteem.

♦   ♦   ♦

When sexual instinct overtakes moral restraint,
a betrayal ensues.

♦   ♦   ♦

Some people can never tell the truth; they habitually
take an addictive drug called amnesia.

♦   ♦   ♦

A big bang trumpeted the baptism of the universe;
the infant is growing into a magnificent adolescent.

♦   ♦   ♦

Lucky are those who act rather than complain.

♦ ♦ ♦

History is written by the conquerors
only if the conquered let them do so.

♦ ♦ ♦

Your candor is a candle in a dark world.

♦ ♦ ♦

This judgment on my literary oeuvre is below
any detestable inconsequentiality.

♦ ♦ ♦

Think of life as an experiment;
we still don't have the findings.

♦ ♦ ♦

My library is a garden teeming
with literary flowers.

♦ ♦ ♦

Weakness courts aggression.

♦ ♦ ♦

For the inexperienced swimmer,
a swimming pool is a potential grave.

♦ ♦ ♦

For every wise advice, there is unwise advice.

♦ ♦ ♦

A big bang was universally heard, proclaiming
the august arrival of the baby universe.

♦ ♦ ♦

War: The resolution of a conflict by violent means!

♦ ♦ ♦

Concise words produce concise meanings.

♦ ♦ ♦

We humans try to protect ourselves in any way we can; in the end though, we are forced to jump off the plane without parachutes.

♦ ♦ ♦

There are limits to nonviolent communication.

♦ ♦ ♦

The inner struggle between certainty and doubt sometimes spills out.

♦ ♦ ♦

Books are vehicles in perpetual motion bearing the fruits of our imagination.

♦ ♦ ♦

Art is the external expression of inner feelings.

♦ ♦ ♦

Pleasing others requires self-denial.

♦ ♦ ♦

Keeping a promise even under dire conditions
is a cardinal virtue.

♦ ♦ ♦

Depriving someone of his inalienable rights
is a cardinal sin.

♦ ♦ ♦

It is easy to say "honor thy mother" until
your mother and your wife have loud arguments.

♦ ♦ ♦

How can a person be accused of blasphemy when he exercises his God-given right to speak up?

♦ ♦ ♦

A hypocrite is one who uses double standards in passing judgments on others.

♦ ♦ ♦

The ugly narcissist: When he sees a reflection on the still pond, he hopes he sees someone else.

♦ ♦ ♦

You cannot break a broken egg.

♦ ♦ ♦

It takes a great deal of skill to write a competent poem with a specific message while not losing its universal validity.

♦ ♦ ♦

Lengthy experiences can be described by a few words, and then distilled into wisdom by even fewer words.

♦ ♦ ♦

An engaged mind is a sound mind.

♦ ♦ ♦

A dormant mind is a dead mind.

♦ ♦ ♦

A handsome face is a passport to unlimited opportunities.

♦ ♦ ♦

Committing a terrorist act against your opponent is politics by other means.

♦ ♦ ♦

Racial intolerance under any circumstances cannot be tolerated.

♦ ♦ ♦

He who refuses to repent when repentance is due shall suffer night and day—in silence.

♦ ♦ ♦

Loch Ness Monster: The probability of its existence does not prove that its existence is probable.

♦ ♦ ♦

Patriotism is patrimony living in our consciousness.

♦　♦　♦

Love is flammable material.

♦　♦　♦

Welcome those who welcome you
and those who initially reject you.

♦　♦　♦

Alliances are meant to be dissolved.

♦　♦　♦

An aphorist is a bugler that wakes a sleepy world.

♦　♦　♦

At its deepest level, love is insusceptible
to logical analysis.

♦ ♦ ♦

Writing an aphorism is an intellectual enjoyment.

♦ ♦ ♦

When you weaponize your feelings,
you hurt others unnecessarily.

♦ ♦ ♦

States hide behind the steel curtain of sovereignty
to commit inexpressible atrocities against humanity.

♦ ♦ ♦

The myth of men being superior to women has been
shattered over and over again;
still, there are pockets of resistance

♦ ♦ ♦

Those who say that wars do not resolve conflicts
are placing their faces in the mud.

♦ ♦ ♦

There is a titanic struggle between what we believe and what we practice.

♦ ♦ ♦

No one alive is completely devoid of ego.

♦ ♦ ♦

Walk softly! The dust we travel on may be the dust of our ancestors.

♦ ♦ ♦

You are now face to face with adversity; you blink, you lose.

♦ ♦ ♦

Illusion is a powerful drug.

♦ ♦ ♦

Keep a flower in your imagination and a humming bird may stop by and say hello.

♦ ♦ ♦

The tragedy of life is its transitoriness.

♦ ♦ ♦

Sometimes the chase is more rewarding than the reward.

♦ ♦ ♦

I am a victim of your excessive magnanimity.

♦ ♦ ♦

Beware of a philosopher's sophistry.

♦ ♦ ♦

Death is big business and the business of death is mournfully costly.

♦ ♦ ♦

One day you hope to be audacious; that day is now.

♦ ♦ ♦

Deprive nations of commerce and you strangle them to death.

♦ ♦ ♦

A progressive moral system is one that respects moral diversity based on universal moral values.

♦ ♦ ♦

To resist adversity is to show moral courage.

♦ ♦ ♦

Give me the means to preserve my dignity
or lead me on the path of martyrdom.

♦ ♦ ♦

Love expressed nonverbally is superior
to love expressed verbally.

♦ ♦ ♦

Do not imitate any one; you would unwittingly
destroy your emerging individuality.

♦ ♦ ♦

As long as a tyrant continues to control the
instruments of power, he has no reason
to loosen his grip.

♦ ♦ ♦

Groupthink is as dangerous as no thinking at all.

♦ ♦ ♦

Groupthink: Choosing collective security over independent thinking and responsibility.

♦ ♦ ♦

My silence is my defense.

♦ ♦ ♦

Human rights transcend democracy.

♦ ♦ ♦

He is a staunch defender of falsehood.

♦ ♦ ♦

When you are chipper, so is everyone around you.

♦ ♦ ♦

Dejection has a way of spreading its effects.

♦ ♦ ♦

Passionless life is not worth living.

♦ ♦ ♦

Those who do not aspire to the future are doomed to live perpetually in the past.

♦ ♦ ♦

If you always act according to your conscience, pretty soon your conscience will be exhausted and traumatized.

♦ ♦ ♦

Nurtured by the right circumstances, even the gentlest human being is capable of committing an unspeakable evil.

◆ ◆ ◆

Judge me not by my words;
words do not convey precision.

◆ ◆ ◆

Faith and fact often clash, so do fact and fact, faith and faith.

◆ ◆ ◆

Pluck petals off a rose and you pluck her quintessence.

◆ ◆ ◆

The dancing wrinkles under your chin are palpable reminders of the beginning of the end.

♦ ♦ ♦

You cannot force an authentic smile out of me until
I change my disposition.

♦ ♦ ♦

Cheerful death may be viewed as an extension of
a cheerful life.

♦ ♦ ♦

You are worth what you think you are worth;
what others think is irrelevant.

♦ ♦ ♦

Those mistakes you make are the foundations
of wisdom.

♦ ♦ ♦

Humanity's most insurmountable affliction is its inability to overcome its proclivity for violence.

♦ ♦ ♦

Traditions chain you to predictable modes of conduct.

♦ ♦ ♦

A puppeteer likes to manipulate his puppet: The human mind.

♦ ♦ ♦

Life is an emergency room, but there is no doctor on duty.

♦ ♦ ♦

Philosophy is the manipulation of abstract ideas to give the impression that it says something of substance.

♦ ♦ ♦

Poetry is a vial containing dubious prophesies.

♦ ♦ ♦

Self-deception is a powerful anesthetic.

♦ ♦ ♦

Aphorism: A Lilliputian that emits nuggets of wisdom.

♦ ♦ ♦

Reason does not necessarily lead to treason.

♦ ♦ ♦

So many women to love, so little hormone left.

♦ ♦ ♦

As life engenders death, death engenders life.

♦ ♦ ♦

You see the fury emanating from my silence;
what will happen next is anybody's guess.

♦ ♦ ♦

Since Time flies, enjoy the ride.

♦ ♦ ♦

Disunited and disgruntled, we fumble and tumble.

♦ ♦ ♦

The birth of fire; the death of innocence.

♦ ♦ ♦

Bereft of spirituality, mankind gropes in the dark.

♦ ♦ ♦

Change is the path of the wise.

♦ ♦ ♦

It is in defeat that one may still shine.

♦ ♦ ♦

What constitutes the human predicament? It is man's inability to predict his posthumous status.

♦ ♦ ♦

Every writer is subversive as he seeks to overthrow existing beliefs.

♦ ♦ ♦

Despite missteps, your ambitions still throb in your brain.

♦ ♦ ♦

Overconfidence is false confidence.

♦ ♦ ♦

Keep dreaming; without a dream, one is bare and destitute.

♦ ♦ ♦

Aspire to achieve the seemingly impossible.

♦ ♦ ♦

If life is precious, why do we continue to develop more lethal weapons in order to kill more people more effectively and en masse?

♦ ♦ ♦

Fear of death is instinctual.

♦ ♦ ♦

Just as there are competing virtues,
there are competing vices.

♦ ♦ ♦

The more powerful countries are,
the less secure they become.

♦ ♦ ♦

What is absent is not known; what is not known
remains absent.

♦ ♦ ♦

To be in love is heavenly; to be out of it is costly.

♦ ♦ ♦

Never let your enemies perceive your weaknesses;
they are waiting to pounce on you.

♦ ♦ ♦

If you cannot survive by wits, bulldoze your way.

♦ ♦ ♦

In poetry, it is essential to leave room
for what is not said.

♦ ♦ ♦

Your deadliest weapon is the big gun you carry;
it is your commitment to the cause.

♦ ♦ ♦

Laws can be liberating or enslaving.

♦ ♦ ♦

What is inaudible in this discussion is the sound
of rationality.

♦   ♦   ♦

I shall not volunteer to step into the sty
of your hatred.

♦   ♦   ♦

This may be your path to paradise,
but it may be someone else's path to perdition.

♦   ♦   ♦

Death is transformative.

♦   ♦   ♦

There is goodness in ugliness, as ugliness
in goodness.

♦   ♦   ♦

We recognize him by his visual absence
and by the presence of his works.

♦ ♦ ♦

Self-control is an acquired art.

♦ ♦ ♦

Patience is power.

♦ ♦ ♦

Beauty sometimes stings.

♦ ♦ ♦

Pay attention to detail as it may hide the answers
to what you are looking for.

♦ ♦ ♦

Patience conquers.

♦ ♦ ♦

If you miss the caravan, there is always the caravansary.

♦ ♦ ♦

War is the lowest rung on the ladder of peace.

♦ ♦ ♦

Beauty and ugliness may not be opposite poles; they offer degrees.

♦ ♦ ♦

Communication: Listen! Listen! Listen!

♦ ♦ ♦

Humility comes from strength of character.

♦ ♦ ♦

By wearing the abaya, you are hiding centuries-old prohibitions.

♦ ♦ ♦

Read history again and again, otherwise it will be rid of you.

♦ ♦ ♦

Biology is amorality.

♦ ♦ ♦

Dogma is a constantly barking dog.

♦ ♦ ♦

Destiny is a final resting place.

♦ ♦ ♦

To fall in love is to fall in the den of courage.

♦ ♦ ♦

The swaying wattle under your chin
is the pendulum of Time.

♦ ♦ ♦

Wealth is an aphrodisiac.

♦ ♦ ♦

Ramming morals into someone's brain
is counterproductive.

♦ ♦ ♦

Experience ascertains the true and the false.

♦ ♦ ♦

Violence is present because authority is absent.

♦ ♦ ♦

Excellence and discipline are symbiotic.

♦ ♦ ♦

These principles are noble. If you do indeed adhere to them, you must be living in a cave way down underground.

♦ ♦ ♦

It is true that some ambitions get burned on the grill of life.

♦ ♦ ♦

We are terminally tethered to this planet.

♦ ♦ ♦

We all complain of life's brevity, but fail to explain the purpose of longevity.

♦ ♦ ♦

Depression is both a natural and psychological phenomenon; so, don't fall into it.

♦ ♦ ♦

When your good looks fade, what crutches do you use?

♦ ♦ ♦

If you fast, you last.

♦ ♦ ♦

Unmitigated, a psychological wound festers with unpredictable consequences.

♦ ♦ ♦

Holding on to the past is seeking reassurance and safety.

♦ ♦ ♦

The human mind is a borderless territory.

♦ ♦ ♦

The scariest thing about your abnormal behavior is that it is normal.

♦ ♦ ♦

The primacy of feeling: I feel before I think.

♦ ♦ ♦

He who thinks he is faultless is boring to a fault.

♦ ♦ ♦

Where prejudice flourishes, violence lies just below the surface.

♦ ♦ ♦

The righteous are lonely people.

♦ ♦ ♦

It must be lonely at the top; it must be lonelier at the bottom.

♦ ♦ ♦

Different kinds of prayers are different kinds of approaches to the same destination.

♦ ♦ ♦

Sleep is suspended death.

♦ ♦ ♦

If you are not an experienced swimmer, your first jump into the deep ocean is your last.

♦ ♦ ♦

In the midst of a crisis, a person's character emerges.

♦ ♦ ♦

Between knowledge and ignorance, there is a territory which you may widen or narrow.

♦ ♦ ♦

Death is an evildoer.

♦ ♦ ♦

Living a life without honor is not worth living.

♦ ♦ ♦

If you are too erotic, you may be erratic.

♦ ♦ ♦

Women do not dress for other women or undress for men; they dress and undress for comfort.

♦ ♦ ♦

Women love power and glamour;
men love to keep them.

♦ ♦ ♦

Challenge and be challenged and
your brain will always be vibrant.

♦ ♦ ♦

Associate with beautiful people and
you will feel their beauty in you.

♦ ♦ ♦

Might is blight.

♦ ♦ ♦

Enthusiasm for action is the enemy of complacency.

♦ ♦ ♦

A wasted mind is a wasted life.

♦ ♦ ♦

We carry the weight of our formative years on our shoulders.

♦ ♦ ♦

Think of yourself less and the world will think more of you.

♦ ♦ ♦

Within a language, there is a pulsating culture.

♦ ♦ ♦

Woe to the truth twister.

♦ ♦ ♦

If you let your body go, it will become your foe.

♦ ♦ ♦

The idea that God is irrelevant is grossly irreverent.

♦ ♦ ♦

The eye is quicker than the mind.

♦ ♦ ♦

We are born strangers and die strangers.

♦ ♦ ♦

The cost of sentimentalism: Oh, the cost of being human.

♦ ♦ ♦

Elegance is acquired, not innate.

♦ ♦ ♦

Humanity is zoology.

♦ ♦ ♦

Since war cannot be abolished, it must be contained.

♦ ♦ ♦

The mystery of life is not equal to the mystery of death; life necessarily ends in death, but death does not end in life.

♦ ♦ ♦

Sometimes the boundary between true and untrue is amorphous.

♦ ♦ ♦

Beauty is indefinable.

♦ ♦ ♦

Words are the external manifestations of internal struggles.

♦ ♦ ♦

Sometimes the winner is the loser.

♦ ♦ ♦

Temptation is the mother of catastrophe.

♦ ♦ ♦

Life is about choices and the choices you make define you.

♦ ♦ ♦

A unified theory of everything alive: Death cannot be disturbed; he is busy doing what he does best.

♦ ♦ ♦

He dies, but his work thrives.

♦ ♦ ♦

The tyranny of unsustainable decrepitude is worse than the tyranny of death.

♦ ♦ ♦

He who woos well shall be well-compensated.

Keep your wallet away from your whims.

♦ ♦ ♦

There are secrets of failure as well as secrets of success.

♦ ♦ ♦

A well-entrenched emotion becomes part of our external look.

♦ ♦ ♦

Power: Love it or leave it

♦ ♦ ♦

Luck: The recognition that forces beyond ourselves are working for us.

♦ ♦ ♦

Keep your heart where it belongs.

♦ ♦ ♦

Most poets are born with their talents; they differ on how they clothe and deliver their works.

♦ ♦ ♦

Let someone perceive you as a weakling and he will walk all over you.

♦ ♦ ♦

A nation devoid of heroes is a nation on the path of extinction.

♦ ♦ ♦

You are the totality of your parts.

♦ ♦ ♦

Good leadership comes from the inside.

♦ ♦ ♦

There is a fine line between you and a buffoon.

♦ ♦ ♦

The most enriching thing a poet can do is not writing, but reading.

♦ ♦ ♦

What was once lounging in the imagination is now standing on the rock of reality.

♦ ♦ ♦

Happiness is an overpriced commodity.

♦ ♦ ♦

No one is beyond reproach, not even saints.

♦ ♦ ♦

The butterfly receives so little time to live, yet it gives so much.

♦ ♦ ♦

If you ignore your past, the past will ignore you.

♦ ♦ ♦

If you don't know your past, you don't know yourself.

♦ ♦ ♦

When winning an argument: Let your opponent feel he has been winning, too. This way you have created a happy loser!

♦ ♦ ♦

If you think life is unfair, wait till you face death.

♦ ♦ ♦

Some leave this planet with good will,
some just the will.

♦ ♦ ♦

The difference between a writer and non-writer is
the former can match ideas with words successfully.

♦ ♦ ♦

Men and women marry, not to defeat loneliness,
but to mollify its effects.

♦ ♦ ♦

The Statue of Liberty is an eternal rhapsody.

♦ ♦ ♦

One's intellect and emotion can never have a rational discussion; their premises are based on different assumptions.

♦ ♦ ♦

Invoking patriotism to defend one's position in a serious intellectual discussion is an attempt to silence an opponent.

♦ ♦ ♦

If a mime was given a gag order by the court, how would he comply?

♦ ♦ ♦

Argumentum ad hominem: Keep your ad hominem tucked away; let us have productive arguments.

♦ ♦ ♦

All this kerfuffle shall benefit no one.

♦ ♦ ♦

I do not bow to catastrophes.

♦ ♦ ♦

An insulated culture is a dying culture.

♦ ♦ ♦

Beyond words and images,
I possess nothing of import.

♦ ♦ ♦

He who woos disasters deserves their furies.

♦ ♦ ♦

All the world is Ellis Island.

♦　♦　♦

We are all immigrants until we reach
our final destinations.

♦　♦　♦

Shall I compare you to the full moon when
I see only a crescent?

♦　♦　♦

There is nothing certain but the palpable
touches of your beloved.

♦　♦　♦

Create wealth and wealth will create your world.

♦　♦　♦

Someone has bequeathed to us this universe.

♦ ♦ ♦

What is not begun cannot be ended.

♦ ♦ ♦

The truth flickers in the pitch dark.

♦ ♦ ♦

An aphorism preserves one's literary legacy in a nutshell.

♦ ♦ ♦

Creativity subverts conventionality.

♦ ♦ ♦

Life is a gambler's paradise.

♦ ♦ ♦

Flaunting ignorance is no virtue.

♦ ♦ ♦

Spewing fumes of hatred will choke us all.

♦ ♦ ♦

Hatred is odious.

♦ ♦ ♦

The moment a politician assumes power,
he assumes the voter is dead.

♦ ♦ ♦

Odor: That the nose knows will not disclose.

♦ ♦ ♦

The price of disunity is incalculable.

♦ ♦ ♦

The price of disunity is the unstaunched flow of suffering.

♦ ♦ ♦

To be sealed in a cultural cocoon is to arrest one's intellectual development.

♦ ♦ ♦

Don't let words lead you to misdeeds.

♦ ♦ ♦

Retirement: It's the end of work days and nights, not the end of life.

♦ ♦ ♦

First impressions stick.

♦ ♦ ♦

You cannot restore broken glass.

♦ ♦ ♦

The key to open doors is to make the key.

♦ ♦ ♦

Witticisms: The reverberations of sharp minds.

♦ ♦ ♦

Death is the granddaddy of all violence.

♦ ♦ ♦

Go to the beach and listen to
what the waves tell you.

♦ ♦ ♦

Selfishness is an integral part of love.

♦ ♦ ♦

Tell the truth without fear because fear distorts it.

♦ ♦ ♦

To be in this world and the next is double jeopardy.

♦ ♦ ♦

Your enemies are but the external manifestations of your inner struggles.

♦ ♦ ♦

Poetry does not create policies for the betterment of mankind, but it illuminates the dark deep potholes one creates.

♦ ♦ ♦

The law cannot indefinitely be sustained while it's being systematically violated.

♦ ♦ ♦

Imagination: Do not leave home without it.

♦ ♦ ♦

My silence inspires hostility, even aggression.

♦ ♦ ♦

Elections: Here we go again; the candidates are dragging bloated sacks of promises.

♦ ♦ ♦

Holders of grand ambitions disdain small ones.

♦ ♦ ♦

Tyranny: The bloodiest tyranny is one that promotes poverty of dreams.

♦ ♦ ♦

Before you correct an injustice by force, correct it by diplomacy.

♦ ♦ ♦

If you don't stop a bully, he will hit you again and again.

♦ ♦ ♦

Love takes you to a higher dimension; lust to a lower one.

♦ ♦ ♦

Sincere love is the sincerest form of bondage between two people.

♦ ♦ ♦

A wise person is one who does not exceed his limitations.

♦ ♦ ♦

Mouth: A portal to health or illness.

♦ ♦ ♦

When your dreams mutate to ashes, let the wind blow them away—and dream anew.

♦ ♦ ♦

Knowledge and ignorance are always in conflict.

♦ ♦ ♦

You may feel strong and confident, but your words are bent twigs.

♦ ♦ ♦

If you don't like yourself, don't act surprised
when people agree with you.

♦ ♦ ♦

He who writes from the depths of his feelings,
shall never die.

♦ ♦ ♦

Behind every successful aphorism,
there is careful editing.

♦ ♦ ♦

What you need is not a psychiatrist,
only the palliative words of a friend.

♦ ♦ ♦

When you are out of work, you're stuck in muck.

♦ ♦ ♦

Raindrops carve stone, make music without
a visible instrument.

♦ ♦ ♦

Diligence deters indigence.

♦ ♦ ♦

He who uses his imagination
can never lose his way.

♦ ♦ ♦

Silence, like any complex language,
presents its own challenges.

♦ ♦ ♦

More reading means more cognitive experiences.

♦ ♦ ♦

Behind every aggression, there is fear.

♦ ♦ ♦

If speech is golden, silence is platinum.

♦ ♦ ♦

I am a measured pessimist.

♦ ♦ ♦

Fueling red-hot anger with more decibels will create more red-hot consequences.

♦ ♦ ♦

Silence is the defense of the intelligent.

♦ ♦ ♦

Weaponizing words further inflames
a flammable situation.

♦ ♦ ♦

Fear none but your conscience.

♦ ♦ ♦

Woe betides those men who claim superiority over
women. Have they given birth to a child?

♦ ♦ ♦

Poetry that brings forth a cliché lasts no longer
than lightning.

♦ ♦ ♦

Seduce someone and you may seduce unwanted
consequences along the way.

♦ ♦ ♦

A synthesis of experiences constitutes knowledge.

♦ ♦ ♦

You go to a psychiatrist for a brain tune-up.

♦ ♦ ♦

Dismantle darkness; install light.

♦ ♦ ♦

The phrase "do good" implies the world is not good.

♦ ♦ ♦

Civilizations always clash.

♦ ♦ ♦

Philosophy starts with questions and ends with more questions.

♦ ♦ ♦

If we stop fighting, we stop living.

♦ ♦ ♦

Dissimilar problems require dissimilar solutions.

♦ ♦ ♦

Maintaining unadulterated virtues is harder than carrying Mount Everest on one's shoulders.

♦ ♦ ♦

It is harder to be than to die.

♦ ♦ ♦

Self-defense is sacrosanct.

♦ ♦ ♦

The burden of love cannot be unburdened.

♦ ♦ ♦

Beauty is the name given to a woman who prefers
not to be called beautiful.

♦ ♦ ♦

Credibility is the name given to one
who is consistent with his beliefs.

♦ ♦ ♦

The ship of Time has anchored; lead me to my
cabin.

♦ ♦ ♦

Wishing to discover truth is the beginning
of self-discovery.

♦ ♦

Liberty undefended is a flight from liberty.

♦ ♦ ♦

When in doubt, don't act.

♦ ♦ ♦

My potbelly is a rest station for my tired calories.

♦ ♦ ♦

Beliefs acquired subliminally are difficult to shake.

♦ ♦ ♦

Be honest all the time and your friends
will abandon you in no time.

♦ ♦ ♦

Sometimes you lose by winning.

♦ ♦ ♦

I have learned much about you by listening to your silence.

♦ ♦ ♦

Indecision may be rooted in deep thinking.

♦ ♦ ♦

Alphabets are not static; they struggle to find meanings for those who manipulate them.

♦ ♦ ♦

A dream is as capable of flying as is the reality of agitating.

♦ ♦ ♦

Let me write in freedom or let me die in dignity.

♦ ♦ ♦

Politicians are reliable liars.

♦ ♦ ♦

It is said that Time flies. Does it have a flight plan? If it does not, how do we track it?

♦ ♦ ♦

Cooking is poetry in heat!

♦ ♦ ♦

A writer reveals himself in his writing—unintentionally.

♦ ♦ ♦

If you wish to lose weight, don't wait.

♦ ♦ ♦

Man is hell-bent on creating monsters of civilization until they consume him.

♦ ♦ ♦

Attach yourself to the certainty of today.

♦ ♦ ♦

Aphorisms are meant to be written and ignored!

♦ ♦ ♦

The assemblage of emotions in this gathering is volatile beyond calculation.

♦ ♦ ♦

Creationism: Case closed.

♦ ♦ ♦

Evolutionism thinks it knows the beginning; the end is an open road.

♦ ♦ ♦

Love and hatred control the world.

♦ ♦ ♦

Falsehood is a language spoken by the desperate.

♦ ♦ ♦

Heaven on Earth is where I live right now; so don't entice me to leave for a hypothetical one.

♦ ♦ ♦

Fatalism is a deadly nail on the coffin of hope.

♦ ♦ ♦

Apartheid: A noose around our physical and spiritual necks.

♦ ♦ ♦

There is no peace without war.

♦ ♦ ♦

A nuclear war will never be fought as long as we believe there is a grain of brain left in us.

♦ ♦ ♦

Sudden wealth is a ladder to unknown heights and lows.

♦ ♦ ♦

It is your business to be a good businessman.

♦ ♦ ♦

Yes, this is a splendid victory, but a victory which sits on a landfill of skeletons.

♦ ♦ ♦

You're a sheep disguised as a tiger.

♦ ♦ ♦

All gloom and groan; no release or relief.

♦ ♦ ♦

Inaction speaks volumes.

♦ ♦ ♦

The fat that settles in my belly is an illegal immigrant.

♦ ♦ ♦

Your so-called literary work is nothing but a hideous monstrosity.

♦ ♦ ♦

Private pain: Suffering absent publicity.

♦ ♦ ♦

Death is the consequence of birth.

♦ ♦ ♦

Coma: Life absent death.

♦ ♦ ♦

I have learned much by listening to my silence.

♦ ♦ ♦

Silence is an expression of involvement.

♦ ♦ ♦

Loopholes are windows of opportunity.

♦ ♦ ♦

What is of consequence now may over time be of inconsequence.

♦ ♦ ♦

Life is a short-term love affair.

♦ ♦ ♦

Conscience bugles and bugles and bugles.

♦ ♦ ♦

Your entreaties shall meet my compassionate nonchalance.

♦ ♦ ♦

Necessity trumps morality.

♦ ♦ ♦

Vice-makers have no colors or currencies.

♦ ♦ ♦

The wheel of history cannot be rolled back.

♦ ♦ ♦

The fear of death is instinctual.

♦ ♦ ♦

There is a fine line between fame and depression.

♦ ♦ ♦

Life is a brief affair with a beautiful woman.

♦ ♦ ♦

Be scandalous and the world will remember you.

♦ ♦ ♦

Death is alive and busy.

♦ ♦ ♦

Sorrowful are the perfectionists.

♦ ♦ ♦

In the heat of battle, those fighters who maintain their principles are indeed the unrecognized heroes.

♦ ♦ ♦

Sprinkle yourself with the perfume
of positive thoughts.

♦ ♦ ♦

What the palate desires may make
the stomach expire.

♦ ♦ ♦

When inferior minds manage to rule,
great minds turn inward.

♦ ♦ ♦

Aging: The physical scourge, the curse of time.

♦ ♦ ♦

Senior sex: Memories of past glories.

♦ ♦ ♦

Stardom: The looming catastrophe.

♦ ♦ ♦

A builder of fortune can also be its destroyer.

♦ ♦ ♦

There is a correlation between suffering
and the flight of conscience.

♦ ♦ ♦

Love can turn the ugliest face into a radiant cherub.

♦ ♦ ♦

Progress is a method of measurement.

♦ ♦ ♦

Diplomacy is the delicate art of manipulation.

♦ ♦ ♦

Love cannot be sustained in a vacuum.

♦ ♦ ♦

Passion rules, reason reigns.

♦ ♦ ♦

Shame is a dungeon invented by righteousness.

♦ ♦ ♦

The past is indomitable.

♦ ♦ ♦

Everyone should be allowed to choose his way to salvation; if this is done, mankind will be spared the scourge of wars.

♦ ♦ ♦

When you're drowning, you cling to anything.

♦ ♦ ♦

If speaking were the only way to communicate, we would be abysmally ignorant.

♦ ♦ ♦

The ladder to fulfillment can also be the ladder to disappointment.

♦ ♦ ♦

Joy of life: Accept what you see and feel.

♦ ♦ ♦

Complacency is a looming cataclysm.

♦ ♦ ♦

Complacency is a ticking bomb.

♦ ♦ ♦

Death is a lonely episode in one's life.

♦ ♦ ♦

Don't knuckle under, knuckle down.

♦ ♦ ♦

When an adversity trammels you,
resist it with patience and hope.

♦ ♦ ♦

Abuse power and power will abuse you.

♦ ♦ ♦

If you believe you will fail, you will.

♦ ♦ ♦

What can be promoted can also be demoted.

♦ ♦ ♦

Actors are vendors of fantasy.

♦ ♦ ♦

Give hatred a chance to die.

♦ ♦ ♦

A hopeless person is a homeless person.

♦ ♦ ♦

Let hope be your vociferous advocate.

♦ ♦ ♦

Work for the common good today;
receive your share tomorrow.

♦ ♦ ♦

Your inner beauty illumines
your fading external beauty.

♦ ♦ ♦

Meet dangers with uncompromising courage.

♦ ♦ ♦

Beware! There are "Hitlers" in all of us.

♦ ♦ ♦

It is more courageous to say "I don't know"
when you really don't know than saying "I know"
when you really don't.

◆ ◆ ◆

The courage to think is not the same
as courage to act.

◆ ◆ ◆

When you restrain a child's speech,
you restrain his imagination.

◆ ◆ ◆

Life is a question mark.

◆ ◆ ◆

The right to question authority is inviolable.

◆ ◆ ◆

Works of art reveal their creators' subterranean dimensions.

♦ ♦ ♦

When there is hope, there is life.

♦ ♦ ♦

To see the facts, shut off your feelings.

♦ ♦ ♦

When you have hope, you have the world.

♦ ♦ ♦

And we will once again survive, even thrive.

♦ ♦ ♦

When you're healthy, you're wealthy.

♦ ♦ ♦

Life is an inquiry into the unknown.

♦ ♦ ♦

Deprivation is the mother of persistence.

♦ ♦ ♦

Fame is fraught with perils.

♦ ♦ ♦

Too much freedom can lead to tyranny,
the tyranny of choice.

♦ ♦ ♦

Indulgence is not free; it is paid for in subtle ways.

♦ ♦ ♦

Life devoid of humor is life devoid of light.

♦ ♦ ♦

Action is mightier than reaction.

♦ ♦ ♦

What is destroyed to its roots cannot be revived.

♦ ♦ ♦

A thin membrane of truth can break
a steel wall of falsehood.

♦ ♦ ♦

Hope is a potent shelter in a turbulent world.

♦ ♦ ♦

When Time speaks, every living creature listens.

♦ ♦ ♦

Time enlightens.

♦ ♦ ♦

Politicians have the gift of gab.

♦ ♦ ♦

Death is terminator of Time.

♦ ♦ ♦

History is an open-ended road.

♦ ♦ ♦

An autodidact is always thirsty for more knowledge.

♦ ♦ ♦

There are places in one's self
that remain unexplored.

♦ ♦ ♦

A butterfly is a beauty chaser.

♦ ♦ ♦

In the heat of battle, truth is in the throes of demise.

♦ ♦ ♦

The roots reach out to other roots—
the entanglement.

♦ ♦ ♦

Water sprinkles here, sprinkles there, and the
sprouts are grateful.

♦ ♦ ♦

Whenever virtue weakens, evil flourishes.

♦ ♦ ♦

In democracy, the rule of law must
be complemented by the role of morality.

♦ ♦ ♦

Optimism is the obverse; pessimism is the reverse
of the same coin.

♦ ♦ ♦

The path to righteousness is strewn with
impediments.

♦ ♦ ♦

Life is a journey without a compass.

♦ ♦ ♦

A person who harbors no hope is a hapless person.

♦ ♦ ♦

Definition of misery: The gulf between our abilities and expectations.

♦ ♦ ♦

A work of art is priceless; it comes from the depths of an artist.

♦ ♦ ♦

Unless bolstered by genuine care,
a relationship is quicksand.

♦ ♦ ♦

Tomorrow is an unending continuation of today.

♦ ♦ ♦

If money is the sole criterion of one's identity,
then its loss is the loss of one's identity.

♦ ♦ ♦

Your future can be entrenched in your past.

♦ ♦ ♦

Birth is a prerequisite of death.

♦ ♦ ♦

Every culture holds its own myths.

♦ ♦ ♦

The power of self-scrutiny cannot be exaggerated.

♦ ♦ ♦

The weight of history is weightier
when you ignore it.

♦ ♦ ♦

The clash between fidelity and infidelity
is a clash of civilizations.

♦ ♦ ♦

To think is to distinguish oneself.

♦ ♦ ♦

Thinking is enlightening.

♦ ♦ ♦

History is a perpetual flame.

♦ ♦ ♦

Hope is the language of the downtrodden.

♦ ♦ ♦

Often, fantasy eclipses reality.

♦ ♦ ♦

Long after war's trenches have been abandoned,
the invisible wounds remain.

♦ ♦ ♦

Musical notes are poetic sounds.

♦ ♦ ♦

Knowledge is certitude.

♦ ♦ ♦

One will forever be known by the words
one leaves behind.

♦ ♦ ♦

In the end, your contrition is the beginning
of your self-realization.

♦ ♦ ♦

The spoken word descends like morning dew
or flies like a bullet.

♦ ♦ ♦

Poetry: Word-wrapped emotions.

♦ ♦ ♦

The roots have not been nourished . . .
the disentanglement.

♦ ♦ ♦

Silence is a siren.

♦　♦　♦

A tradition may not be as oppressive
as its practitioner.

♦　♦　♦

He who knows himself knows the world.

♦　♦　♦

Hope does not just fall in your lap; you must
stir it to action.

♦　♦　♦

When one buys an original painting,
one creates an orphan.

♦　♦　♦

Self-control is an immeasurable virtue.

♦ ♦ ♦

Greatness and genius are interrelated.

♦ ♦ ♦

Money is a silent executioner.

♦ ♦ ♦

I have heard the bombast, but have not seen the muscles.

♦ ♦ ♦

Verbosity is the enemy of brevity.

♦ ♦ ♦

History reflects what humanity has wrought.

♦ ♦ ♦

History boasts of its unfettered power

♦ ♦ ♦

Procrastinators play with fire.

♦ ♦ ♦

Like diseases, prejudices are contractible.

♦ ♦ ♦

Kindness is balm.

♦ ♦ ♦

When fatalism becomes entrenched, recovery is doomed.

♦ ♦ ♦

A dead conscience cannot be lured back to life.

♦ ♦ ♦

Power is perilous and less of it is still perilous.

♦ ♦ ♦

Terrorism is a symptom of a larger ailment.

♦ ♦ ♦

The more a liar lies, the more lies
he has to remember.

♦ ♦ ♦

Illumine the path with compassion
and people will always seek you.

♦ ♦ ♦

Beware of sycophants; they can ruin your day.

♦ ♦ ♦

Life is not a perennial symphony;
allow for an occasional disharmony.

♦ ♦ ♦

To fulfill a dream, one must travel long and hard.

♦ ♦ ♦

Learn to live and vice versa.

♦ ♦ ♦

Where arrogance of power remains unrestrained,
people shall succumb.

♦ ♦ ♦

Your future starts with your past.

♦ ♦ ♦

Expand your horizons by being a rebel,
a nonconformist.

♦ ♦ ♦

Money is labor of love, so it should
not be squandered.

♦ ♦ ♦

Empathy does not necessarily generate sympathy.

♦ ♦ ♦

When one is hungry, someone else is overfed.

♦ ♦ ♦

Perfection is not an achievable goal.

♦ ♦ ♦

In any human enterprise, initiative is paramount.

♦ ♦ ♦

Our psychology determines our thoughts.

♦ ♦ ♦

In the beginning, there was nothing;
in the end there will be nothing.

♦ ♦ ♦

There is safety in silence.

♦ ♦ ♦

A philosopher is an untiring seeker of knowledge
and wisdom.

♦ ♦ ♦

Life is impermanent; death permanent.

♦ ♦ ♦

Mother Nature invades my privacy,
offers no apology, and scurries away.

♦ ♦ ♦

The Sphinx declares: I am immortality!

♦ ♦ ♦

Freedom to know is akin to the unblocked
blood flow.

♦ ♦ ♦

The more you tenaciously adhere to your principles,
the more ideologically-entrenched you become.

♦ ♦ ♦

Every popular revolution must lead to the sovereignty of the people.

♦ ♦ ♦

What is far may actually be near.

♦ ♦ ♦

Paper money reflects the illusion of its face value.

♦ ♦ ♦

Civilizations do clash.

♦ ♦ ♦

A stagnant civilization is a dying civilization.

♦ ♦ ♦

If love were absent, we would look for it.

♦ ♦ ♦

You cannot restrain the vociferous rooster at dawn anymore than you can restrain the sprawling colors of dawn.

♦ ♦ ♦

The holy is folly when taken to the extreme.

♦ ♦ ♦

If animals were able to write their autobiographies, their abusers would fill planets.

♦ ♦ ♦

Like the human mind, the vast pathless desert is not empty; it will reveal treasures and surprises.

♦ ♦ ♦

Love possessed, love abused.

♦ ♦ ♦

Lend me your silence and I will read your thoughts!

♦ ♦ ♦

My soulless supposed soul mate further degenerates into irrelevance.

♦ ♦ ♦

The wise do not have a monopoly on wisdom.

♦ ♦ ♦

We all shall trudge to our beginnings.

♦ ♦ ♦

Curiosity can save your life.

♦ ♦ ♦

Low self-esteem is as dangerous as a ticking bomb.

♦ ♦ ♦

A mime speaks wordlessly—and eloquently.

♦ ♦ ♦

We cannot subdue a turbulent ocean,
but we can circumvent its schemes.

♦ ♦ ♦

Think what you will, but bear the consequences.

♦ ♦ ♦

The end makes a new beginning possible.

♦ ♦ ♦

Bereft of charisma, beauty soon fades.

♦ ♦ ♦

You pay for your unrestrained emotions.

♦ ♦ ♦

An intellectual is one who could not care less about feelings until he feels deprived of his primal needs.

♦ ♦ ♦

Hope is the discovery of an alternative to despair.

♦ ♦ ♦

Think today; reap tomorrow.

♦ ♦ ♦

Friends and foes compete for your attention,
although for different motives.

♦ ♦ ♦

My writing bares my soul;
my silence bears my burden.

♦ ♦ ♦

Combat some one's angry words
with palliative ones.

♦ ♦ ♦

A poet is a cricket that sounds his thoughts
in the wilderness of night.

♦ ♦ ♦

Sadly, progress sometimes cannot be made
without violence.

♦ ♦ ♦

Feelings cannot be neutralized.

♦ ♦ ♦

Don't live on the opinions of others.

♦ ♦ ♦

Try to catch two slithering snakes simultaneously, and you will catch neither.

♦ ♦ ♦

The angrier you are, the less stable you become.

♦ ♦ ♦

Two chefs in the same kitchen at the same time will cook a disaster.

♦ ♦ ♦

There is a symbiosis between religious fundamentalism and totalitarianism.

♦ ♦ ♦

Power is gender-neutral.

♦ ♦ ♦

If you don't know what you want from life, then you don't need a strategy.

♦ ♦ ♦

When compassion is lacking, people perish.

♦ ♦ ♦

Opprobrium cannot be erased by anger or protestation.

♦ ♦ ♦

Your birthmark is your signature.

♦ ♦ ♦

Dissipated love, like dissipated heat, is costly.

♦ ♦ ♦

War is the vehicle of the feeble-minded.

♦ ♦ ♦

War is the instrument of the unimaginative.

♦ ♦ ♦

War sees the victor sit on a pile of ashes.

♦ ♦ ♦

The fearless shall inherit the world.

♦ ♦ ♦

An agitated person cannot make a rational decision.

♦ ♦ ♦

To democratize philanthropy is to enhance mankind's communal interests.

♦ ♦ ♦

If you want to preserve your life, persevere.

♦ ♦ ♦

We are born frail; we die frail.

♦ ♦ ♦

When one's strength diminishes, one's desperation spikes.

♦ ♦ ♦

Philosophy cannot be divorced from its audacious inquisitiveness.

♦ ♦ ♦

Suffering predates thought.

♦ ♦ ♦

Principled men tolerate no compromise.

♦ ♦ ♦

Patriotism does not include brutalizing your enemies.

♦ ♦ ♦

Depending on your own behavior, your enemy can become your friend.

♦ ♦ ♦

If you cannot divide and rule, then deprive and rule.

♦ ♦ ♦

Money saved is money spent,
but without losing sight of it.

♦ ♦ ♦

Mediocre is a name cherished by those
who have limited vision.

♦ ♦ ♦

Hope points out hope as her solace.

♦ ♦ ♦

Mr. Politician, you're dragging the country
to the slaughterhouse.

♦ ♦ ♦

Creative minds are fond of sabotaging traditions.

♦ ♦ ♦

One cannot counsel or discipline
the spiritually dead.

♦ ♦ ♦

One is free to think, but not to act.

♦ ♦ ♦

Success cannot be attained in a vacuum.

♦ ♦ ♦

Flowers never die.

♦ ♦ ♦

If you're convinced you're right,
then right what is not right.

♦ ♦ ♦

In war, conscience is silent.

♦ ♦ ♦

Every colonizer leaves behind his stench.

♦ ♦ ♦

When youth dims, wisdom emerges.

♦ ♦ ♦

My silence is my response, loud and clear.

♦ ♦ ♦

The sound of water is the sound of life.

♦ ♦ ♦

You're persuasive even if you don't say anything.

♦ ♦ ♦

Alas, what you see in the mirror is really you.

♦ ♦ ♦

I am unsure as to whether the medicine
is collaborating with the disease.

♦ ♦ ♦

Hope is timeless.

♦ ♦ ♦

Hope is a flame that cannot be extinguished.

♦ ♦ ♦

Hope is a dove that never stops cooing.

♦ ♦ ♦

Hopelessness is not a language used by hope.

♦ ♦ ♦

Hope is an ointment that can be rubbed
on the wound of the sufferer.

♦ ♦ ♦

With hope, today's hardship will ease tomorrow.

♦ ♦ ♦

Hope is an incessant drumbeat.

♦ ♦ ♦

Hope is perennially incandescent.

♦ ♦ ♦

Hope is feeling that things will turn around.

♦ ♦ ♦

We are all arrested in this universe,
but free to roam in it!

♦ ♦ ♦

You're poor if you have poor attitudes.

♦ ♦ ♦

Power: Use it advisedly or lose it gracefully.

♦ ♦ ♦

If you don't like to be criticized,
don't show off your writings.

♦ ♦ ♦

If you are attuned to public approval,
you're no longer attuned to your principles.

♦ ♦ ♦

The world is a living museum.

♦ ♦ ♦

The world is a botanical garden.

♦ ♦ ♦

Intolerance breeds intolerance.

♦ ♦ ♦

Intolerance bleeds tolerance.

♦ ♦ ♦

Aphorisms should be lived, not preached.

♦ ♦ ♦

A turbulent mind sees only a turbulent world.

♦ ♦ ♦

We all have darkness in us.

♦ ♦ ♦

To be born, to be forlorn.

♦ ♦ ♦

Life is a bridge to nowhere.

♦ ♦ ♦

The only constant in the equation of life is death.

♦ ♦ ♦

All of us are entitled to display an
occasional stupidity.

♦ ♦ ♦

Think before you proceed.

♦ ♦ ♦

Abandoning rules means abdicating responsibility.

♦ ♦ ♦

Hunger of the body stupefies the mind.

♦ ♦ ♦

The whine in the quiet of dawn
is the loud cry of despondency.

♦ ♦ ♦

Expand your intellectual horizons
by thinking critically and often.

♦ ♦ ♦

In the context of the universe, no one in this planet
is a failure.

♦ ♦ ♦

Progress is a universal language.

♦ ♦ ♦

Extreme poverty leads to extreme brevity of life.

♦ ♦ ♦

It is less costly to love than to hate.

♦ ♦ ♦

Truth is lilting.

♦ ♦ ♦

Be as graceful in defeat as in victory.

♦ ♦ ♦

Beware! What you proudly grow
can turn against you.

♦ ♦ ♦

My aphorisms are my spokesmen.

♦ ♦ ♦

If you seek glory, you will have to contend
with inglorious nights and days.

♦ ♦ ♦

Ignorance is a pestilence.

♦ ♦ ♦

Abstinence makes you more sensitive
to deprivation.

♦ ♦ ♦

If you flaunt your beauty now and nothing else,
what will you flaunt when you are 100?

♦ ♦ ♦

Beware! The voice of your vice is getting louder
than the voice of your virtue.

♦ ♦ ♦

As long as you have an imagination, the word
"impossible" should not be a part
of your vocabulary.

♦ ♦ ♦

Life is theatre of the abstruse.

♦ ♦ ♦

The mind cannot indefinitely restrain
one's galloping hormones.

♦ ♦ ♦

Democracy allows irreverence.

♦ ♦ ♦

The truth eventually will agitate for freedom.

♦ ♦ ♦

Watch out! Words are flaming spears.

♦ ♦ ♦

Dreams are patchworks of unreality.

♦ ♦ ♦

What you're subliminally exposed to will affect your behavior all your life.

♦ ♦ ♦

The misdeeds you commit will forever live within you.

♦ ♦ ♦

Be at the proximity of power,
and your own power will grow immeasurably.

♦ ♦ ♦

Celibacy is bliss; marriage is courage.

♦ ♦ ♦

After the chaos of revolution:
The state of law is the state sought.

♦ ♦ ♦

Leadership: Sustained vigilance and initiative.

♦ ♦ ♦

An effective conflict resolution strategy
comes from an effective management style.

♦ ♦ ♦

Emotions drive the body.

♦ ♦ ♦

History is the receptor, not the creator.

♦ ♦ ♦

Today's gift is better than tomorrow's promise.

♦ ♦ ♦

Politics is the intellectual handmaiden of war.

♦ ♦ ♦

The mind keeps erecting barriers
to avoid telling the truth.

♦ ♦ ♦

Ignore your conscience at your peril.

♦ ♦ ♦

Small gains will produce large triumphs.

♦ ♦ ♦

Sound judgments come from lengthy ruminations.

♦ ♦ ♦

When a woman's beauty fades,
she summons her experiences.

♦ ♦ ♦

War is amoral.

♦ ♦ ♦

In war, only bullets speak.

♦ ♦ ♦

A matador is a metaphor for
humanity's inhumanity.

♦ ♦ ♦

A religion is but a restraint on the volatility of human behavior.

♦ ♦ ♦

Let your words ripen on the vine of wisdom.

♦ ♦ ♦

Money is a vehicle which observes no traffic rules.

♦ ♦ ♦

What attracts you to her? It's not the obvious.

♦ ♦ ♦

You cannot force someone to sleep.

♦ ♦ ♦

Stability comes from change.

♦ ♦ ♦

An aphorism is a mechanism to jell your thoughts into a practical guide.

♦ ♦ ♦

The power of your absence is overwhelming.

♦ ♦ ♦

The internet is the new temple.

♦ ♦ ♦

Loneliness is bad company.

♦ ♦ ♦

If you are able to pull me by my sentimental rear, you own me.

♦ ♦ ♦

The most insufferable thing is to deny one
the acquisition of knowledge.

♦ ♦ ♦

Everyone has a story to tell and a legacy to leave.

♦ ♦ ♦

A metaphor is in the mind of the beholder.

♦ ♦ ♦

Disorganization is the enemy of progress.

♦ ♦ ♦

To question authority is to be assertive,
to question oneself is to display personal courage.

♦ ♦ ♦

Fear of pain produces pain.

♦ ♦ ♦

Like an ego, a fire is harmless until you touch it.

♦ ♦ ♦

When a butterfly flutters, she unknowingly stirs emotions deep inside us.

♦ ♦ ♦

Your imagination is an inexhaustible source of inspiration.

♦ ♦ ♦

If you insist on finding happiness, you will never find it.

♦ ♦ ♦

Honesty is the worst policy if you are a diplomat or a politician.

♦ ♦ ♦

If you can fly in your imaginary raft, you are on solid ground.

♦ ♦ ♦

Laws should not and cannot be devoid of moral values.

♦ ♦ ♦

Experiences consist of gold and dross; it's your choice.

♦ ♦ ♦

Education is subversion of the existing order.

♦ ♦ ♦

Words are carriers of thoughts;
they are beasts of burden.

♦ ♦ ♦

No antagonism as intense as one between
truth and untruth.

♦ ♦ ♦

Blaming someone else for your mistake
is incontestably diabolical.

♦ ♦ ♦

I am seized by unceasing ebullience
every time I see you.

♦ ♦ ♦

What we eat determines our shape.

♦ ♦ ♦

Your beauty robs the mind of its oxygen.

♦ ♦ ♦

Moderate defense of freedom is unsustainable.

♦ ♦ ♦

The perils of imprudence cannot be exaggerated.

♦ ♦ ♦

Sometimes it takes a nudge to start a serious action.

♦ ♦ ♦

Part of your personality is formed
by what you're exposed to subliminally.

♦ ♦ ♦

Life is a never-ending rhythm.

♦ ♦ ♦

Competition is self-promotion,
a desire to be triumphal.

♦ ♦ ♦

The best offence is when the enemy is indulged
in over-confidence.

♦ ♦ ♦

The universe is poetry read
in slow deliberate notions.

♦ ♦ ♦

Where immoderacy is the norm of the group,
stay away.

♦ ♦ ♦

The words you use reveal your biography.

♦ ♦ ♦

Studied efforts will produce ingenious solutions.

♦ ♦ ♦

Questioning your faith will ultimately strengthen it,

♦ ♦ ♦

Under pressure, don't scream like a siren;
bleat like a sheep or tweet like a bird.

♦ ♦ ♦

The reproductive organs are endowed with the
power to continue or discontinue the human race.

♦ ♦ ♦

Character develops on the grill of daily strife.

♦ ♦ ♦

Shedding your tears means dispelling
your inner toxins.

♦ ♦ ♦

Youth are susceptible to youthful indiscretions;
the old, the frailties of decrepitude.

♦ ♦ ♦

What is a figment of the imagination today
will be concrete reality tomorrow.

♦ ♦ ♦

Don't avail yourself of tragedy.

♦ ♦ ♦

Freedom is an inner, unending struggle.

♦ ♦ ♦

Essentially, what lifts you and me lifts humanity.

INDEX

"do good", 185
"Hitlers", 205
abaya, 152
abnormal behavior, 156
Abraham Lincoln, 57
absent, 87, 147, 153
abstinence, 248
abuse, 44
accomplishments, 74
achievement, 30
act, 124, 139, 181, 188, 238
action, 61, 160, 209
actors, 204
adversity, 134, 136, 203
affliction, 40, 141
age, 50, 74, 76
aggression, 126, 178, 183
aging, 199
agitated person, 235
agrees, 108
air, 22, 119
alive, 94
alliances, 132
ally, 24
alphabets, 189

altruism, 47
ambiguity, 24
ambition, 43, 89, 106
ambitions, 25, 145, 154, 178
ancestors, 134
anger, 40, 107, 183, 233
angrier, 232
angry words, 231
animals, 90, 227
apartheid, 193
aphorism, 133, 143, 173, 181, 255
aphorisms, 81, 99, 191, 244, 247
aphorist, 58, 132
aphoristically, 68
argument, 7, 21
argumentum, 170
arrogance, 222
art, 13, 47, 108, 119, 128, 150
art for art's sake, 119
art of lying, 108
aspire, 146
assertive, 41
atheism, 45, 103
attracts, 108, 254

audacious, 136
audacity, 66
authentic smile, 141
autodidact, 210
bank, 69, 70
battle of the sexes, 93
battles, 121
beach, 176
beautiful people, 159
beautiful woman, 18
beauty, 3, 17, 23, 36, 45, 51, 62, 67, 72, 83, 87, 108, 118, 150, 151, 159, 163, 187, 211, 230, 248, 253, 260
beginning, 71, 140, 187, 192, 217, 224, 229
beginnings, 228
behave young, 57
behavior, 14, 26, 36, 46, 66, 98, 100
behind closed doors, 110
being human, 162
belief, 5
beliefs, 188
believe, 3, 54, 134, 193, 204
belong, 62
best, 34, 69, 74, 93, 114

Beware!, 64, 111, 205, 247, 248
biblical, 36
big bang, 124, 126
bigotry, 119
biography, 262
biology, 123, 152
birth, 1, 86, 95, 144, 184, 195, 214
birth of humanity, 86
blaming, 259
blasphemy, 129
blood flow, 225
bombast, 219
book, 31, 40, 105, 115
books, 95, 127
born, 8, 26, 161, 166, 235, 244
boundary, 163
bow, 171
brain, 107, 145, 153, 159
brain tune-up, 185
brains, 68
broken egg, 129
broken glass, 176
brutal events, 94
bully, 179
burden of love, 187
businessman, 24, 193
butterfly, 168, 211, 257
candor, 125

cantankerous, 56
caravan, 151
cardinal sin, 128
cardinal virtue, 128
carrots and a big stick, 83
carry on, 54
catastrophe, 15
celibacy, 251
certain, 50, 84
certainty, 86, 127, 191
challenges, 109, 182
change, 39, 66, 106, 115, 141, 145, 255
character, 29, 74, 151, 158, 263
charisma, 230
chase, 135
chefs, 232
child's speech, 206
children, 19, 76, 104
chipper, 138
choices, 164
civilization, 80, 115, 191
civilizations, 13, 185, 226
clash, 140, 185, 215, 226
cleavage, 83
cliché, 66, 110, 184
cocoon, 175
colonizer, 239

coma, 195
comedian, 55
commerce, 136
common good, 205
communicate, 202
communication, 70, 127, 151
compassion, 221, 233
competent poem, 129
competition, 261
complacency, 202, 203
composure, 74
comprehension, 94
conflict resolution, 116, 251
conformity, 8
conscience, 80, 139, 184, 196, 200, 239, 252
consequence, 195, 196
consequences, 9, 28, 32, 82
continuation, 95, 213
contradictions, 27
contrition, 217
convictions, 40
cooking, 190
cornucopia, 63
cost, 39, 40, 45
counsel, 238
courageous, 206

crab, 99
creationism, 191
creative minds, 238
creativity, 2, 66, 115, 173
creator, 18
credibility, 187
crescent, 172
criticisms, 53
criticized, 243
crossed the bridge, 56
cry, 85, 246
culture, 52, 161, 171, 214
curiosity, 83, 228
cynics, 75
dancing wrinkles, 140
dangerous, 41, 64, 97, 100, 137
dangers, 205
dark, 4, 50, 57, 72
darkness, 185, 244
Darwin, 90
dead conscience, 221
death, 1, 10, 42, 49, 50, 64, 77, 85, 101, 107, 115, 116, 136, 141, 143, 144, 146, 149, 157, 158, 162, 164, 169, 176, 195, 197, 198, 203, 210, 214, 225, 245
deeds, 31
defeat, 1, 109, 145, 169, 247
defense, 21, 32
defy the world, 102
dejection, 139
democracy, 62, 97, 138, 212, 249
demoted, 204
depression, 155
deprivation, 208
depths, 19
despair, 34, 230
destiny, 152
destroyed, 209
destruction-construction, 26
detail, 150
details, 13
deviating from your planned route, 22
diamond rule, 112
dictator, 49, 64
die, 10, 53, 94, 161, 164
diet, 92
different, 13
dignity, 15, 124, 137
diligence, 182
diplomacy, 201
disappointment, 202
disaster, 37, 84
disasters, 171
disbelieve, 54

discipline, 72, 154, 238
disease, 100, 240
disentanglement, 217
disorganization, 256
distortion, 13
disunited, 144
disunity, 174, 175
divide and rule, 237
dogma, 152
dormant mind, 130
double jeopardy, 177
doubt, 86, 119, 127, 188
dove, 241
dream, 146, 180, 189, 222
dreams, 25, 45, 179, 180, 250
drowning, 202
drunk, 99
earth, 85
earthly bliss, 121
East and West, 79
eat, 260
ebullience, 259
education, 25, 65, 77, 92, 103, 258
effort, 16, 94, 110
ego, 109, 134, 257
elections, 178
elegance, 162
Ellis Island, 171

emotion, 165
emotional, 18, 60, 87
emotions, 54, 78, 191, 217, 230, 251
empathy, 223
end, 64, 71, 127, 140, 162, 175, 192, 217, 224, 229
enemies, 19, 27, 114, 147, 177, 236
enemy, 20, 24, 160, 219, 236
engaged mind, 130
entanglement, 211
entreaties, 197
envy, 27, 38
equation of life, 245
erotic, 159
etiquette, 27
evil, 23, 30, 65, 73, 113, 116, 212
evil people, 113
evolutionism, 192
excellence, 66, 154
exceptionalist, 110
existence of evil, 116
expect, 48
experience, 3, 4, 14, 17, 67, 86, 153
experiences, 3, 28, 88, 92, 130, 182, 185, 253, 258
external beauty, 205

eye, 36, 84, 113, 161
eyes, 36, 38
fact, 5, 6
facts, 15, 103, 207
Facts, 28
fail, 90, 154, 204
fair, 95
fairness, 114
faith and fact, 140
falsehood, 29, 33, 138, 192, 209
fame, 81, 91, 208
fame and depression, 197
fanatic, 14
fantasy, 1, 204, 216
far, 226
fast, 2, 155
fat, 194
fatalism, 192, 220
faultless, 156
fear, 11, 16, 17, 63, 83, 89, 146, 184
fearless, 234
feel, 13, 16, 46, 78
feeling, 21, 30, 68, 156
feelings, 36, 68, 71, 113, 133, 181, 207, 230, 232
feelings and thoughts, 113
femaleness, 79

fiction, 72, 89
fidelity, 215
fighting, 186
figment, 263
fine line, 167
fire, 69, 89, 144, 220, 257
fish, 101
flame, 215, 240
flaunt, 248
Flaunting, 27
florist, 58
flower, 4, 10, 89, 135
flowers, 238
foe, 161
foes, 231
folly, 227
fool, 3, 86
force, 141, 179, 254
formative years, 160
fortune, 200
frail, 235
Franklin, 76
free expression, 106
free verse, 16
freedom, 26, 114, 190, 208, 225, 249, 260, 264
freedom of expression, 114
friend, 59, 69, 70, 89, 181, 236
friends, 87, 98, 231

frugal, 41
fulfillment, 79, 89, 202
full moon, 172
fury, 144
future, 20, 28, 37, 62, 91, 139, 214, 222
galloping hormones, 249
give, 88, 107, 137
gloom and groan, 194
glories, 11
glory, 247
God, 129, 161
good, 24, 36, 54, 65, 69, 73, 77, 96
good diplomat, 69
good looks, 155
good will, 169
goodness, 36, 149
gossiping, 115
grandeur, 71
great minds, 199
great poet, 59
great poetry, 48, 60
greatness, 219
greed, 104
greedy, 6
ground, 21, 46, 79, 89, 101, 104
groupthink, 86, 137, 138
gun, 88

hand, 15, 28
handsome face, 130
happiness, 16, 35, 39, 60, 120, 167, 257
hasty, 28
hate, 247
hatred, 9, 38, 48, 149, 174, 204
have little, 49
hazards of living, 103
healing, 85
health, 34
healthy, 207
hear, 38
heart, 52, 71, 166
heat of battle, 198, 211
heaven, 122, 192
Heaven and Hades, 122
heifers, 95
heights, 11
heroes, 52, 166
histories, 93
history, 8, 22, 37, 51, 111, 123, 125, 152, 197, 210, 215, 219, 220, 251
holy, 227
home, 86
homeless, 204
honest, 188
honesty, 258

hope, 53, 74, 107,
  109, 136, 192, 203,
  204, 207, 209, 213,
  216, 218, 230, 237,
  240, 241, 242
hopeful, 120
hopeless, 204
hopelessness, 241
horizons, 223, 246
hormone, 143
human, 3, 13, 15, 18,
  26, 64, 73, 75, 87,
  95, 105, 122, 139,
  142, 145
human behavior, 3
human life, 122
human nature, 37
human race, 75
human rights, 138
humanitarian, 75
humanity, 29, 33, 46,
  59, 61, 70, 99, 117,
  118, 133, 141, 162
humans, 1, 14, 16, 51,
  122, 127
humility, 43, 116
humor, 111, 209
hunger, 245
hungry, 223
hurt, 7
hydrant, 69
hypocrite, 6, 129
idea, 69

idealist, 87
identity, 31, 214
ignoble, 8
ignorance, 5, 35, 39,
  173, 248
ignorant, 24, 54
illusion, 3, 134
imaginary raft, 258
imagination, 2, 4, 63,
  67, 127, 135, 178,
  182, 206, 249, 257,
  263
imagine, 91
imitate, 137
immigrants, 172
immoderacy, 261
immortal, 67
immortalized, 53
impatient, 90
impossible, 120, 146
impressions, 175
imprudence, 260
in the imagination,
  167
inaction, 194
inconsequence, 196
indecision, 114, 189
indigence, 5
individuality, 50
individually, 59
indulgence, 208
infant, 31
inferior minds, 199

infidelity, 215
initiative, 224, 251
injustice, 85, 179
inner beauty, 205
inner feelings, 128
inner paradise, 118
inner struggle, 127
inner toxins, 263
innocents, 99
insecurity, 11
inspiration, 39, 257
instinctual, 99, 146
intellect and emotion, 170
intellectual, 13, 60, 91, 133, 170, 175, 230, 246, 252
intellectual activity, 13
internet, 255
intimacy, 90
intolerance, 243
intuition, 79
invent, 14
journey, 54, 55, 120, 212
joy of life, 202
judgment, 125
judgments, 28, 129, 253
justice, 36, 49, 94
kerfuffle, 100, 170
key, 176

kindness, 220
kitten, 48
knowledge, 4, 5, 25, 27, 67, 88, 117, 158, 180, 185, 210, 216, 224, 256
knowledge and ignorance, 158, 180
knows himself, 218
knuckle down, 203
lamppost, 57
language, 7, 112, 161
language skills, 112
law, 17, 178, 212, 251
laws, 12, 60, 122, 148, 258
laws of nature, 12
leader, 74
leadership, 113, 167, 251
learn to live, 222
leave this earth, 42
legacy, 173, 256
less, 56, 117, 147, 160
lethal, 92
liar, 221
liberty, 52, 59, 81, 109, 188
library, 63, 125
life, 1, 2, 8, 14, 18, 19, 22, 23, 27, 28, 31, 38, 41, 48, 59, 61, 64, 65, 74, 78,

87, 94, 95, 98, 101, 107, 111, 112, 115, 121, 125, 135, 139, 141, 142, 143, 146, 154, 158, 160, 162, 164, 169, 173, 175, 195, 196, 198, 203, 206, 207, 208, 209, 212, 221, 222, 225, 228, 233, 235, 239, 244, 246, 249, 250, 261
light, 49, 76, 185, 209
like, 20, 21, 22, 43, 55, 68, 69, 76, 106, 107, 181, 182, 217, 234, 243
limitation, 115
literary work, 195
literary works, 88
Loch Ness Monster, 131
logic, 73
loneliness, 255
lonely, 9, 157
loopholes, 196
love, 2, 8, 19, 45, 48, 56, 57, 78, 79, 89, 102, 132, 137, 143, 147, 152, 159, 165, 177, 179, 196, 200, 201, 223, 227, 228, 234, 247

love affair, 196
love and hatred, 192
lovers, 77
luck, 165
lucky, 124
lust, 179
machine, 122
magnanimity, 135
majesty, 71
man, 6, 15, 18, 73, 75
man and a woman, 65
mankind, 44, 56, 105, 144
marriage, 20, 22, 117, 251
matador, 253
medicine, 23, 100, 240
mediocre, 237
mediocrity, 66
meditation, 6
memory, 14, 34, 96, 106
men, 19, 45, 54, 83, 100, 133
men and women, 169
metaphor, 253, 256
middle age, 68
might, 160
mime, 170, 229
mind, 6, 7, 10, 15, 28, 39, 55, 58, 82, 84, 96, 103, 117, 130,

142, 156, 161, 227, 244, 245, 249, 252
mirror, 105, 240
mirth, 8
misdeeds, 175, 250
misery, 8, 118, 213
mistakes, 11, 90, 141
moderation, 66
monarchy, 97
money, 23, 70, 98, 219, 223, 237, 254
moral, 17
moral system, 136
moral values, 136, 258
morality, 5, 60
morals, 76, 153
mortal, 67
mother, 128
Mother Nature, 225
Mother Theresa, 115
mouth, 180
Mr. Politician, 237
muscles, 219
museum, 243
mystery, 162
myth, 133
narcissist, 129
nationalism, 42, 97
nature, 11, 26, 29
near, 42, 226
necessity, 197
new ideas, 57

noble, 8, 21
not begun, 173
notes, 216
nuclear war, 193
ocean, 13, 43, 79, 158, 229
odor, 174
offense, 32
old, 33, 57, 152, 263
old age, 18
older, 7, 19
opinions, 31, 52, 232
opportunity, 196
opprobrium, 233
optimism, 77, 212
optimistic, 75
opulence, 5
orphan, 218
our own sun, 119
out of work, 181
outgoing, 62
overconfidence, 146
over-confidence, 261
pain, 257
painful, 111
painting, 218
palate, 199
paleontology, 47
palliative words, 181
palpable touches, 172
paper money, 226
paradise, 121, 149
partial answers, 43

passion, 15, 100, 201
past, 34, 39, 139, 156, 168, 199, 201, 214, 222
pathless desert, 227
patience, 55, 150
patient, 90
patriotism, 21, 33, 36, 131, 170, 236
peace, 43, 151, 193
peak of the mountain, 61
perceive, 147, 166
perdition, 149
perfection, 223
perfectionists, 198
persevere, 235
person, 6, 7, 11, 12, 17, 23, 29, 76, 105, 108, 129
personality, 260
persuasive, 240
pessimism, 35, 212
pessimist, 183
philanthropy, 235
philosopher, 88, 224
philosophy, 142, 185, 236
pit bull, 22
placebo, 85
places, 81, 211
planet, 20, 26, 104, 154
podiatrist, 93
poem, 33, 56, 98, 108
poet, 16, 23, 167, 231
poet of peace, 112
poetry, 3, 9, 15, 16, 23, 30, 37, 48, 51, 63, 111, 142, 148, 177, 184, 217
poets, 11, 166
poise, 87
political leaders, 41
politician, 174
politicians, 190, 210
politics, 20, 131, 252
poor, 19, 34, 242
positive attitude, 72
positive thinking, 84
positive thoughts, 199
possess, 53
possessions, 11, 98, 117
possessiveness, 122
possible, 120
potbelly, 188
poverty, 66, 179, 246
power, 5, 20, 51, 60, 70, 116, 137, 150, 159, 165, 174, 203, 214, 220, 221, 222, 233, 242, 250
power of your absence, 255

powerful countries, 147
practice, 134
prayer, 6
prayers, 157
predicament, 122, 145
predictable, 46
prejudice, 157
prejudices, 220
pride, 12
principled men, 236
principles, 17, 30, 54, 70, 154, 198, 225, 243
private pain, 195
probability, 131
problems, 43, 186
procrastinators, 220
progress, 15, 56, 200, 231, 246
promoted, 204
prose, 63
protein, 91
psychology, 224
public approval, 243
puppeteer, 142
question, 32, 206, 256
question authority, 206
racial intolerance, 131
radical, 90
raindrops, 182
rational, 18, 87

rational being, 18
reaction, 83, 209
read, 14
reading, 167, 182
reality, 1, 13, 80, 167, 189, 216, 263
reason, 137, 143, 201
rebel, 223
relationship, 65, 90, 213
religion, 44, 54, 82, 254
repent, 131
repentance, 102, 131
reproductive organs, 262
reputation, 7
resources, 12
respect, 71, 73
responsibility, 86, 245
retirement, 175
reunion, 81
revisit the past, 32
revolution, 226, 251
riches, 19, 91
right, 55, 129, 139, 192, 206, 239
righteous, 157
rights, 35
romancing, 21
rooster, 227
roots, 209, 211, 217
rose, 39, 45, 62, 140

rosebud, 2
roses, 36
rules, 97, 101, 201, 245, 254
ruminate, 123
rumor, 6, 111
rush, 36
saints, 168
salvation, 93, 201
sanctuary, 69, 86
scandalous, 198
science, 80, 82
sea, 5, 41, 71
secrets, 165
security, 3
seduce, 184
seduction, 120
see, 18, 38
see the world, 46
seeking, 32, 156
self-acceptance, 113
self-analysis, 64
self-control, 55, 150, 218
self-deception, 143
self-defense, 186
self-denial, 30, 128
self-discovery, 123, 187
self-esteem, 102, 124, 229
selfishness, 177
self-knowledge, 74

self-love, 102
self-realization, 217
self-recovery, 15
self-respect, 71, 73
self-scrutiny, 214
senile, 100
senior sex, 199
sentimental, 255
sentimentalism, 73, 162
serious action, 260
sex, 19
sexual instinct, 124
shallows, 19
shame, 201
sheep, 194
silence, 7, 23, 63, 84, 131, 138, 144, 170, 178, 182, 183, 195, 196, 217, 224, 228, 231, 239
simple lifestyle, 121
sin, 33, 35
sincere love, 179
skepticism, 25
sky, 71
slander, 41
sleep, 37, 68, 98, 157, 254
snakes, 232
social skills, 76
socialism, 97
society, 8, 34

soliloquy, 65
solitude, 7
sophistry, 135
soul, 4, 17, 33
soul mate, 228
sound of rationality, 148
sounds, 216, 231
speech, 183
Sphinx, 225
spiritual, 23, 80, 89
spirituality, 144
spoken word, 217
Stability, 255
stagnant civilization, 226
stands, 42, 101, 106
stardom, 200
states, 133
Statue of Liberty, 169
staunch defender, 138
stomach, 199
story, 256
strangers, 161
strength, 151, 235
strong and confident, 180
studied efforts, 262
stupid, 105
stupidity, 111, 245
subliminally, 188, 250
subtle beauty, 95
subversion, 25, 258
success, 118, 238
suffering, 23, 28, 70, 99, 120, 175, 195, 200, 236
sunset, 64
superiority, 184
supreme purpose, 85
surprises, 227
survive, 89, 102, 148, 207
swim, 19, 41, 79
swimmer, 126, 158
sycophants, 221
symbiosis, 233
system of beliefs, 29
tact, 75
teach, 12
tears, 9, 56, 263
temperance, 11
temple, 55
temptation, 21, 76, 81, 104, 163
terrorism, 221
terrorist act, 131
theater, 96
theism, 103
these thoughts, 37
think, 46, 52, 59, 93, 125, 141, 156, 160, 169, 215, 229, 230, 238, 245
thinking, 215
thorn, 10

thought, 3, 19, 30, 58, 61, 66
thoughtful, 44
thoughtfulness, 64
thoughts, 6, 59, 70, 77, 82, 224, 228, 231, 255, 259
thrive, 89, 207
tiger, 194
time, 5, 6, 7, 9, 12, 17, 21, 26, 42, 58, 69, 78, 79, 94, 96, 106, 144, 153, 187, 190, 210
to be, 19, 26, 30, 31, 37, 39, 41, 44, 50, 81, 86, 93, 96, 97, 100, 120, 132, 136, 147, 186, 191, 193, 243, 244
to die, 186, 204
to err, 55
today, 8, 37, 62, 191, 205, 213, 230, 241, 252
tolerance, 50, 119
tombstone, 56
tomorrow, 8, 205, 230, 241, 252
totality, 166
tradition, 218
traditional marriage, 108
traditions, 15, 142
tragedy, 55, 86, 96, 135, 263
tranquility, 60, 82, 91
traumatized, 108, 139
Traveling, 22, 46
treasures, 227
triumphs, 252
true love, 6, 78
trust, 24, 117
truth, 5, 8, 26, 29, 33, 42, 51, 72, 82, 89, 105, 106, 107, 109, 111, 114, 124, 161, 173, 177, 187, 209, 211, 247, 249, 252, 259
tyranny, 15, 164, 179, 208
tyrant, 137
UFO, 91
ugliness, 36, 149, 151
uncertainty, 84
under pressure, 262
unexpected, 48
unexplored, 211
unfair, 34, 169
unified theory, 164
universe, 10, 17, 94, 124, 126, 172, 242, 246, 261
unknown, 83
unspeakable evil, 139

untruth, 82, 259
unwise, 126
validity, 18
value, 19
verbal calisthenics, 112
verbosity, 219
verses and ideas, 58
vibrant, 102, 159
vice, 2, 4, 116
vice-makers, 197
vices, 147
victim, 135
victory, 109, 194, 247
violence, 102, 121, 141, 153, 157, 176, 231
virtue, 2, 4, 116
virtues, 147, 186
visit, 20, 32, 39, 40
visual absence, 149
voice of your vice, 248
war, 29, 44, 61, 126, 151, 162, 193, 216, 234, 239, 252, 253
warm feeling, 40
wars, 33, 36, 44, 46, 121, 133, 201
wasted mind, 160
water, 87, 116, 211, 239
wattle, 153

weak, 85, 97
weakling, 166
weakness, 44, 126
weaknesses, 12
wealth, 23, 34, 47, 60, 71, 153, 172, 193
wealthy, 34
weapon, 107, 148
weight, 160, 191
weight of history, 215
welcome, 132
what I am about, 112
what you see, 100
whims, 118, 165
whine, 246
wife, 128
win, 7, 45, 65
winds, 118
winner, 51, 163
winning, 168, 189
winning an argument, 168
wisdom, 9, 11, 14, 42, 46, 53, 103, 105, 110, 130, 141, 143, 224, 228, 239, 254
wise, 101, 126, 145
wise person, 180
wishes, 11, 53
without honor, 158
wits, 12, 148
witticisms, 176
woe, 161

womb, 17
women, 19, 45, 83, 133, 143, 159, 184
woos, 164, 171
words, 9, 10, 31, 33, 37, 58, 63, 77, 82, 92, 98, 103, 105, 116, 117, 121, 127, 130, 140, 163, 169, 171, 175, 180, 184, 216, 250, 254, 259
words and images, 171
work, 56, 78, 93
work of art, 69, 213
works of art, 207
world, 48, 57, 61, 75, 82, 83, 90, 99, 109, 112, 125, 132, 160, 171, 172, 177, 185, 192, 198, 207, 209, 218, 234, 243, 244
world government, 66

worst, 114
worth, 30, 65, 93, 139, 141
wound, 111, 155
wounds, 43, 78, 85, 98, 216
write, 56, 95
writer, 50, 95, 145, 169, 190
writes, 63, 89, 181
writing, 9, 15, 37, 63, 68, 167, 190, 231
writings, 243
younger, 19
your birthmark, 234
your faith, 262
your mistakes, 109
your silence, 189
yourself, 122, 123, 160, 168, 181, 191, 199
youth, 239, 263

ACKNOWLEDGMENTS

My profound gratitude goes to my life-long partner Judith Ann Herrick for her unstinting support and encouragement in the preparation of this manuscript.

I would also like to thank poet Ibrahim Ibn Salma for his thoughtful and challenging remarks.

BIOGRAPHY

Mahdy Y. Khaiyat holds degrees from the University of California, Santa Barbara, and is a freelance editor and translator.

He started writing poetry in 1990. The publication of his first poem in a literary magazine in the same year encouraged him to continue writing. His poems have since been published in periodicals in the United States, Canada, Australia, France, Japan, Belgium, England, Finland, and Argentina.

Three years ago, he began writing aphorisms. This book is a compilation of many of those sparking conversations. The readers can draw their own conclusions and begin their own conversations.

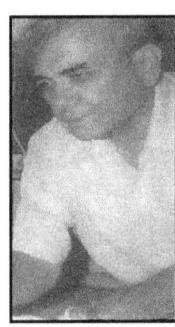

www.ingramcontent.com/pod-product-compliance
Lightning Source LLC
Chambersburg PA
CBHW031620160426
43196CB00006B/207